To Roma

Hope you find

interesting & may you ...

The Case
Against Reincarnation

A Rational Approach

With Good Wishes

James Webster

3rd Oct. 2011

by

James Webster

Grosvenor House
Publishing Limited

This book is published by
Grosvenor House Publishing Ltd
28-30 High Street, Guildford, Surrey, GU1 3HY.
www.grosvenorhousepublishing.co.uk

A CIP record for this book
is available from the British Library

ISBN 978-1-906645-93-9

Also by James Webster

'Life Is ForEver' *A personal investigation for evidence of survival (Woodside Publications 2000 Reprinted 2003) ISBN: 0-9538073-0-4*

Contents

Acknowledgements

I would like to thank most sincerely all those who have so kindly made the writing of this book possible by granting me permission to quote and copy, so generously, from their work and material. I also thank my wife for her time and patience with editing and offering sound advice and some valuable comments. Also grateful thanks to my brother Tony who draw up the fine original cartoons, with his artistic talent, to include in my book.

Whilst writing I am so often aware of those in the finer spirit world around me, helping and inspiring me, so much. They so often pop just the right words and ideas into my mind. So my special thanks to all those friends and loved ones wherever they abide.

I also wish to acknowledge the following organisations and associations for their informative help:

Bahá'í Reference Library (Agency of the Bahá'í International Community)
The Christian Parapsychologist
Colin Fry Enterprises Ltd
Confraternity of Faithists (Kosmon Church)
Greater World Christian Spiritualist Association
Krishnamurti Foundation Trust
Psychic News
Psychic World
Spiritualists National Union

Introduction

The idea of returning to Earth – this physical world – to spend further lifetimes, appeals to, and is accepted by, a very large and increasing number of the world population. There is a saying; *If you shout loud enough and long enough you will be believed and accepted* and I think it was Winston Churchill who said, or stated something like; *A majority vote does not necessarily make it right.* This is how it has been with the reincarnationists and their theory which has been so promoted and accepted by so many, that it is no longer recognised by them as a theory, but more as a <u>proven fact</u> by the way in which they treat it.

There are many reasons for the popularity of reincarnation as indeed on the surface it does seem to answer certain questions of injustice and offers some ways and means of repaying debts through what is often known as *karma.*

Some find it quite impossible to think in terms of facing an unknown spirit life after physical death, and would prefer – as they see it – the 'comfort' of coming back to live further lives in a world and environment they have been used to and acquainted with, in another physical body. Although this preference is questionable, and can only refer to the minority, rather than to all those who have experienced a dreadful or impaired existence, as so many millions have and do. In the East, particularly, they resign themselves to it and just accept without question as part of their karmic and religious belief and teaching.

Many fear or just accept that death of the physical body marks the end of existence altogether and resign themselves to that belief.

Millions are attached to the Eastern religions of Buddhism and Hinduism which teach reincarnation as a prime tenet. Many other religions, sects and cults also promote reincarnation as a prime part of their teaching. Brainwashing from birth, by the doctrine, leads to and becomes an entrenched belief system.

Throughout my professional life I have met and spoken with so many people – some as patients and some as friends or acquaintances. So often questions arise and conversations begin on the deeper aspects concerning life and death. I have been quite amazed as to how many are quite surprised when I say that I do not accept reincarnation. Even those with an often somewhat limited interest (the newspaper horoscopes or an occasional visit to a medium or psychic etc.) unwittingly hang on to a kind of acceptance, without questioning, of the theory of physical re-birth as fact or at least as the most likely consequence. The media are also much to blame for this 'brainwashing' because they are just as gullible and, in general, uninformed.

Although many people hate the idea of returning again to the earth, they seem to see it more as a 'normal happening', punishment or consequence over which they have no control. Some would prefer to be dead and gone forever. There is so much fear and uncertainty in people mainly through lack of proper education on the subject.

My own research into survival (life after death) covers some fifty years and I have to confess that at some stage, during earlier research, in my innocence, I too accepted and believed in reincarnation, as it appeared at the time to answer certain prime questions – or so I thought. I also held the notions that I may have lived at least one past-life on Earth. However, my views changed quite dramatically when the time was right, and I began some further more in-depth research.

Discovering that reincarnation belief was not only a myth and erroneous in its normally universal orthodox teaching, I realised that many of those researching it and expounding it were attempting to make it a gateway for proving survival and would sooner or later have to face the fact that the <u>very reverse</u> was the case.

Although I have no problem with survival of the individual conscious personality, I do have problems – not with myself – but with those who cling on to their belief in reincarnation and just cannot quite let it go completely.

Even some today who call or label themselves *Spiritualists* – including certain mediums – will insist on accepting the doctrine of reincarnation and alleged past-lives as their belief and even teach it. One cannot be a *Spiritualist* <u>and</u> *Reincarnationist* without being a hypocrite! There is no alliance between true Spiritualism and reincarnation as the reader will discover later on in this book when I refer to some of the great and fine pioneers and what they had to say.

I propose to take the reader, and venture together into this maze, and successfully find a way out to at least some clearer understanding.

Many books have been written on the subject of reincarnation and alleged past-lives, supporting the belief and attempting to turn theory into fact. Also many have been written by those 'on the fence' attempting to put the case 'for' and 'against' the theory leaving it open ended and inconclusive through lack of researched and essential information, thus leaving the reader just as perplexed in having to make up their own mind.

My intention in this book is to fundamentally place the case firmly **against** the theory and doctrine as it is most usually presented and taught in its orthodox and dogmatic way. It is impossible to prove a negative and it is certainly not my intention to attempt to do so. In my presentation I will examine the weaknesses and doubts which are so often taken on board by the protagonists and prevalent with the 'don't knows' and offer, not only my own thoughts and interpretations, but chiefly those of others who have far better qualifications in certain areas than have I. These include scientists, philosophers, religionists and teachers from a wide field past and present.

I hope those who consider that being re-born again and again into this earthly life existence, for any reason or not, will find this book 'food for thought'.

Although I respect every person's <u>right</u> to their beliefs I do not necessarily respect their <u>beliefs.</u>

Personally I look forward to the next stage of the progressive journey through the etheric and finer spirit planes where **all** the opportunities – including the missed ones – are really made available to each and every one of us. I quote a fine and profound teacher communicating from the next world who said:

> *'You have not begun to live—*
> *You do not know what living is'*

James Webster
Battle, East Sussex

CHAPTER 1

Reincarnation – The Tender Trap

The idea and belief of returning again to earth after the demise of the physical body and living through anything from a few, to hundreds or thousands of re-births or re-incarnations, has been a doctrine held for many centuries particularly by the Eastern religions. In the West the belief has gathered pace particularly with the emergence of the so called *New-Age* with its many appendages.

On the surface, reincarnation does seem to answer so many questions concerning inequality and injustice and the learning of lessons, but that is the deception. Most of those who teach the doctrine will insist that one life, however long, is not enough to learn the lessons and experiences of earth. They will insist and teach that we have to return to put right the wrong doings of our previous life or lives through what is known as karma. This may involve a change of gender, experiencing pain and suffering, misfortune and a never ending list of other requirements.

Many mediums and psychics have jumped on the bandwagon in recent years realising that the gullible public are prepared to part with their money too easily and be told some fairy tale about who they had been in an alleged previous life on earth, and why they were reaping or suffering this time around. There is no way of proving what they are told of course. That is the get-out clause!

All kinds of quasi-therapies have come into fashion with no authentic or scientific backing. One such is hypno-regression often carried out by unqualified people. This is both unreliable and can have dangerous consequences. Hypnosis for medical purposes practiced by qualified practitioners is a different matter. I am speaking here about those who experiment by attempting to regress a client to a supposed(?) <u>past-life before birth.</u> Very unhealthy indeed and should not be practiced by either the unqualified or qualified for reasons made clearer later on in this book.

Many will remember back in early 1999, when popular ex-professional footballer and now football manager and coach Glenn Hoddle, was in the public news and received considerable media attention in the press and television which nearly ruined his career. His entanglement with the healer and reincarnationist Eileen Drewery caused the trouble when it was revealed that they held the belief that children born deformed and handicapped <u>chose</u> to come back in that state through the consequences of their past-life and were evidently paying back bad karma. This caused an uproar and outrage all over the country especially from the handicapped and disabled Societies.

There are so many bizarre and wretched cases on record referring to and involving past-life, karmic and reincarnation belief. Thousands of cults and sects have mushroomed in Britain, America and other parts of the world of quasi-religious structure mostly incorporating these beliefs. They can so often appear to be attractive and illuminating to the unaware and unprepared, before they are trapped.

At this point it is probably a good idea to set out, with some quotes included, what it is the reincarnationist is mostly prepared to accept in their belief. This will depend largely upon whether they follow the tenets of a religion or religious sect, a cult, Theosophy, Spiritism or hold no label or following, apart from a general acceptance of the theory.

The following is an extract taken from a website of someone following Hinduism. It confirms yet again some of the appalling beliefs held by the reincarnationists:

'................ People who believe in reincarnation say you have had many lives before your present life and will have many lives after your present life.

.......Poverty, crime, pain and suffering plays a part of all our lives in some way or another. Ever questioned as to why these things exist? Why is there so much evil in this world? Why do innocent people suffer? God as we know it is all-good and all-powerful, then why are little children suffering from poverty and hunger? This can be explained by the Hindu's belief in Karma. The idea of Karma states that one suffers because he is being punished for his past sins. Therefore, if a 2-year-old has a deadly disease, the child is paying for all his wrongful acts from his past life. God is all-good; therefore he would not bring evil into the world and tolerate the suffering of innocent people unless they deserved to be punished.

.......Since God is all-powerful, He would be able to destroy the deadly disease from an infant and as stated before He would not tolerate the suffering of an innocent person. Since God does not destroy evil from the world, it's safe to say that people who suffer deserve to suffer because they are paying for a sin they committed in their previous life.'

From another website:

Reincarnation: Some people being punished in this life-time for their persecution of Christians in Ancient Rome.

'It's a great misfortune to have a disability or an incurable disease. While seeing that others are healthy and full of energy, these people can only endure excruciating pain brought about by their illness. People often complain to the heavens for the injustice they seem to suffer. They ask: 'Why do I have to suffer misfortune?'

Regarding these 'injustices', cultivators think they are the result of evil deeds committed in previous lives. In other words, people live many lives and their karma (a substance created by doing bad things) is connected with afflictions and illnesses in this life. In the West, many doctors and scholars have been able to find out (*allegedly*) about patients' previous lives and thus determine the true cause of their pains and sicknesses in this life.

In her book *Many Mansions – The Edgar Cayce Story on Reincarnation*, Dr. Gina Cerminara lists examples of treating patients through readings of their previous lives by Edgar Cayce (1877-1945), a famous American psychic. Edgar Cayce had the ability to give 'readings' on patients who were thousands of miles away after he entered into a self-induced sleep state.

Among the many cases 'read' by Edgar Cayce, some were traced back to the ancient Roman Empire. Some of the patients in these cases participated (*allegedly*) in the persecution against Christians, directly or indirectly.

One of them was a 45-year-old woman. She was paralyzed by polio at the age of 36 and had to rely on a wheelchair to get around. After unsuccessfully trying many treatments, she found Cayce and asked him to give her a reading of her previous lives. She learned that the reason for her paralysis in this life was what she had done in ancient Rome. Between 37-68AD, she was a member of the Royal Court when Emperor Nero persecuted Christians. She not only had no sympathy for the Christians who were mutilated in the Coliseum, but she also sneered at them. The price for her cold sneers was to be paralyzed in this life.

Another patient was a girl. She was an aristocrat in her previous life during Nero's rule, and she enjoyed watching Christians being tortured in the Coliseum. She even laughed loudly when she saw a young girl's body torn apart by a lion. This aristocrat who took pleasure in martyrs' sufferings was paying back her sins with tuberculosis.

Another case involved a movie producer who suffered from polio at the age of 17. He had a slight limp from his bad foot. During the reading of his previous lives, Cayce found that this person had also participated in persecution against Christians. He was a soldier at the time and was ordered to persecute Christians, who did not fight back. His sin was not the result of obeying his orders as a soldier, but of sneering at people who persisted in their faith. His disability in this life was meant to awaken him.

The last patient was a boy. His back was injured in a car accident when he was 16, and he lost all feeling from below the fifth vertebra. He could not move and had to rely on a wheelchair. Seven and a half years later, when he was 23 years old, his mother asked Cayce to do a reading for him, and two of his previous lives were read. One of them showed him as a soldier in the ancient Roman Empire during the early period of the persecution against Christianity. He was very conceited and took pleasure in the Christians' sufferings. He also directly participated in the persecution. And so he had to endure pain in this life.

The readings on these people indicated the true cause of their pain and suffering – they used to laugh at and persecute people who persisted in their faith. At the same time, the readings show that behind the superficial illness-causing elements, an invisible force that exists on an unknown and deeper level is controlling peoples fates. It also supports the old Chinese proverb; *Good is rewarded with good, evil is met with evil.* That is not merely a saying. Although the patients in the first two cases did not directly participate in the persecutions, they did not support the righteous. So they had to pay with suffering for their ignorance and coldness in previous lives. As for those who were directly involved in the persecution, exemplified by the fourth patient, they had to endure excruciating pain even at a young age.'

There was no possible way of proving any of these cases. Cayce meanwhile was, no doubt, making a good living out of it!

Many others today are also making a good living from these so called *mediumistic/psychic readings* and causing much mental disturbance to the gullible who fall into their trap!

CHAPTER 2

Pioneer Spiritualist

Harry Boddington

These are the publisher's comments on the back cover of the book *The University of Spiritualism* by Harry Boddington:

The origin of this authoritative book is a three-year course on all aspects of Spiritualism that was prepared by the author for students.

He spent over 40 years in its preparation. It involved studying comparative religion, science, philosophy, ethics, logic and political economy.

The result, which he rightly regarded as the crown of his life's work, is a comprehensive study of Spiritualism in all its manifold aspects.

The author was one of London's pioneer Spiritualists. He devoted practically all his time to writing and lecturing on Spiritualism and became one of its most knowledgeable exponents.

He read every worthwhile book dealing with psychic matters. He witnessed every phase of psychic phenomena. Moreover, being married to a brilliant medium, he had many unique opportunities of making first-hand investigations into psychic happenings, especially, when at their most intriguing and impressive occasions, they came spontaneously.

The final result is a fascinating work from a man who was a brilliant thinker with the gift of lucid exposition, ably qualified to be the 'Head' of the University of Spiritualism.

I include this excerpt from Chapter xvii

THE PROBLEM OF REINCARNATION

With the advent of modern Spiritualism, occultists of various types emerged from their hiding-places to attack the common enemy. They particularly objected to the analysis of mental states which separates subconscious activity from external mentalities, while recognising the operations of both. They found their preserves invaded, their adepts reduced to the level of ordinary mediums, and cherished 'secrets' broadcast and explained. Led by Madame Blavatsky, they retaliated by threatening all mediums – not developed by their 'adepts' – with vampirism, and loudly proclaimed that all Spiritualists were liable to become obsessed by spook shells and elementals. Spiritualists laughed at them, and continue laughing, because many have been raised from beds of sickness by the very powers who were supposed to be contemplating their destruction. But the lie has had a long start, and can only be defeated by continual repudiation. Madame Blavatsky's writings form the main source of information accepted by her followers.

The 'adepts' affect a lofty intellectualism which resents critical analysis, and prevents truth emerging. They profess to despise the 'simple' explanations of Spiritualism, and quite fail to grasp the significant fact that truth is wonderfully simple, although simply wonderful. Their chief claim to intellectuality, arises from memorising eastern words and phrases, which, without a knowledge of mediumship to interpret them, are simply empty jargon. They massed their forces under the banner of the Theosophical Society; but time is wreaking its revenge. Many mediums, in the hope of learning more perfect methods of development, joined their lodges and speedily pricked the bubble of inflated ignorance. Their association left a distinctive mark upon the more progressive minds, and many Theosophists, like Mrs. Besant, have said that good as well as bad influences 'may' at times communicate. Occultists unite to 'damn with faint praise' all mediumship that they do not personally develop. As in the Church of Rome, the exception arises when a psychic experience falls to the lot of one of their own followers. Then, as in the case of Madame Blavatsky, or the saints, it is not mediumship, but something mysterious and far more wonderful. Their fulminations on the 'dangers' of mediumship, on examination, are found to be childishly imaginative. Once the mind realises its own creative powers and knows that it can build up phantasms with which primitive man scared himself, all occult terrors fade away.

The most casual study of hypnotism clarifies the issue because the inquirer knows that his mental attitude, plus psychic adaptability, accounts for all phenomena, both in the seance room and occultism. Secret societies have a knack of discovering one another. An interchange of 'secrets' naturally follows. In this way Freemasonry has been laid under tribute, but each group differs from its kindred in the special emphasis and value attached to the symbols used. Many seem to make a compound of all the superstitions they can collect, and weird and fantastic are the only words that adequately describe many 'occult' ceremonies. He who would invoke the uncanny forces first draws a circle around himself to keep at a (mental) distance powers he is obviously afraid of. In the circle, and around it, are his cabalistic signs. The magical formula is then pronounced – usually a meaningless word like 'abracadabra' – intermixed with jargon modernised to suit the mentality of the audience. Sometimes a slight measure of psychic power possessed by one of the members lends colour to the theory adopted, but usually the most appalling ignorance of elementary mediumship and auto-suggestion is exhibited. Secrecy and mysticism are prolific breeding-grounds for fear and terrorism, and it is here that harpies, blackmailers and dogmatisers find fullest expression.

The creation of a reincarnated Jesus in the person of Krishnamurti – after considerable training – and the rise of a new priesthood with inner (esoteric) and outer (exoteric) rules and regulations was but the natural outcome. The same gaudy show that attracts Roman Catholics was imitated in order that the same result of keeping the masses (exoteric section) in ignorance follows. But when Krishnamurti went on strike, this house of cards fell.

Against secrecy of all kinds, Spiritualism wages incessant warfare. Science is a better leader than slavish fear, even though for the moment orthodox scientists may be our antagonists. Mankind has an inherent tendency to accept loudly asserted authority, but Spiritualists consistently refuse to accept the fables of occultists in place of ascertained fact. By proving the much-vaunted dangers to be non-existent, psychical research has cleared the way for rational communication between the two worlds. The mental imagery on which fears were based has been scientifically demolished and spirit communion rescued from obloquy and oblivion. This in turn has destroyed the idea that the soul at death splits up into sections with neither the will nor the ability to communicate with earth peoples. Spiritualists find themselves co-operating with wise and loving counsellors only, and never see or hear of the weird speculations called spook shells or elementals whom occultists presume to control. We learn, instead, that in the spirit realms purity of thought and desire to help are greater powers than academic teaching; that the higher mentalities control the lower, and we have no wish, even if it were remotely possible, to ally ourselves to states of consciousness so degrading as projecting, building or controlling vicious elemental forces.

Occultism was presumably driven underground by the fearful persecutions of Rome in the Dark Ages, when all natural psychics were burned or tortured by the 'Holy' Inquisition as wizards or witches. They crushed the message-bearers and prevented the manifestations of the holy 'comforters' promised by Jesus, and in addition produced the very wizardry they so much feared. For when natural faculties may only be exercised in secret, they tend to become distorted and perverted. Abuse rather than right use always results. One has but to listen to the assumptions of Theosophists when talking about mediumship to realise the utterly ridiculous depths to which dogmatic assertion can fall. If you do not believe in reincarnation, you are plainly told you are an unevolved soul, and therefore cannot develop psychic power, and for nearly a century there have been stories of vampires upon unsuspecting mediums and wreaking untold misery.

Unfortunately for the theory, mediums prove to be a healthier class of people than any others, and make health their special study in order to develop sane mediumship. So we are unmoved by the constant repetition of threats. Experience is the best teacher. But it is necessary to repeat these statements over and over again, because the lie has had a long start, and Madame Blavatsky is still the main authority for statements that are quoted.

A Theosophic leader was asked at our study group who or what it was that mediums saw when they described spirit people whose separate individuality they are able to prove in many ways. The medium who put the question was gravely told that her spirit guides were probably her own individuality masquerading under four different personalities. In other words, her spirit guides were all lying one against the other, although the medium is normally a most truthful person. This type of present-day Theosophist has quite innocently swallowed 'Blavatskyism' with the same unthinking credulity that accepts creedalism at a mother's knee. Many are confused by the teaching that, after death, man divides up into sections, and that the mental portion gets far away from all earthly considerations, while the astral counterpart of the physical slowly disintegrates, and the section that clairvoyants see is an etheric shell that flits about graveyards or bobs up at seance rooms until in time it also disintegrates. Neither the astral nor etheric portions have any consciousness of their own, and are said to squeeze some semblance of consciousness out of mediums. Theosophists thus endow the unconscious with greater power than the conscious, and grotesquely exaggerate all theories of sub-conscious activity, rather than accept spirit control. Only a mahatma – a man still living in a physical body with his seven vehicles (bodies) intact – could perform the miracles of the seance room. Many occult theories revolve around this idea.

Their other dilemma hinges on the doctrine of reincarnation. Many Theosophists readily accept the statements of any spirit who teaches reincarnation, but repudiate all others. The doctrine of reincarnation conduces to obsession, because its believers cling tenaciously to the idea that the earth is their future dwelling-place. They thus mentally chain themselves to it in their hunt for a human body to possess. They regard the earth as the only place where full consciousness is expressed, because each section of the seven bodies at death is believed to take a portion of the mentality with it, and never reincarnates with its previous sections.

Occultists are split up into numerous antagonistic groups, but unite to attack Spiritualism. What Spence's *Encyclopaedia of Occultism* thinks about Madame Blavatsky may be gathered from the following extract: 'She was well known in America as a Spiritualistic medium.' (I pause at this point to emphasise a fact persistently denied by her followers.) 'Madame Blavatsky was the daughter of a Russian colonel. She twice entered Tibet, and, finding it exceedingly difficult and dangerous to do so, probably decided her to adopt it as the home of the mahatmas or great masters. These were presumed to be gigantic intellects who have mastered the yoga philosophy and are able to leave their bodies at will. The idea was exploded when explorers discovered the savage nature of the Tibetans, quite the opposite of her assumptions. Since that time new localities are being found for the 'great masters', mostly in India, where it is easy to keep up the deception.'

(The evidence for the existence of mahatmas rests mainly upon the statements of three or four people who may, or may not, have been deceived.)

Her teaching may be summarised thus: Man at death splits up into etheric, astral, mental, intuitional, spiritual, nomadic and divine sections. Each is supplied with a body separate and distinct from its fellows, which eventually gets absorbed into other forms of life. Individuality in the physical sense is impossible to the discarnate spirit. As the various sections decay, that part of the nature dies also. Finally, an emasculated mentality seeks reincarnation.

Theosophists are hard pressed to find explanations for the conclusive evidence for spirit identities of the seance room, and explain it by peopling the spirit world with thought-images called elementals. These have no consciousness of their own, but borrow it from the medium's thoughts. The impertinence which assumes that all mediums are deceived and only the assumptions of Theosophists are correct, the assumptions of absolute ignorance, needs no refutation; it defeats its own ends. They claim that Theosophic seers go into the spirit world and get their information at first hand, and that spirit mediums are misled by elementals. It is unfortunate for Theosophy that the majority of its seers see nothing clairvoyantly until the illusion is created by the 'instructions of their masters.' In other words, auto-suggestion is the basis of most of their visions. The main defect of reincarnation lies in the fact that nature produces one spirit associated with the form it first manifests through. In order to accommodate the doctrine of reincarnation, this primitive and original spirit is pushed on one side in order to make way for spirit number two, who was originally born like spirit number one, but now dispenses with the process. Nature never stultifies herself in that way.

On the death of Madame Blavatsky in 1891, there was a bitter struggle for leadership, during which charges of fraud, hallucination, and even less desirable epithets were freely bandied about. In the resulting split, W.Q. Judge retained the leadership of the American section, succeeded by Catherine Tingley: while Mrs. Annie Besant with Colonel Olcott remained heads of the English and Indian sections. These are still bitterly hostile to each other, but the British Indian section contains elements which are slowly emancipating themselves from the literal acceptance of Madame Blavatsky's assertions and partly embracing Spiritualistic ideals and theories. Olcott's *Old Diary Leaves* reveals Madame Blavatsky's mediumship quite clearly. He shows how she was used for automatic writing, but, instead of ordinary spirit control, he claimed it was control by a mahatma or great master who still possessed an earthly body. Spiritualists have often duplicated this form of spirit control, and deny that it proves Madame Blavatsky's claims. Frederic Bligh Bond, in the American *Journal of Psychical Research* for 1929, gives a very clear instance of receiving automatic script from a friend still on earth, who gave full name and details, which Bligh Bond checked on returning to England, thus proving that it is not necessary to pass through the change of death before we can act as spirit controls.

That Madame Blavatsky's controls were great 'masters' we have every reason to doubt, since William Emmett Colman traced many of her teachings to existing literature. Spiritualists who watched her career know that a very ordinary woman's jealousy prompted most of the utterances that her followers today produce as evidence against mediumship. This was confirmed by her letter to the *Pall Mall Gazette* in 1884, in which she proclaimed her mission to 'put down Spiritualism.' Unfortunately, 'the written word remaineth,' and Spiritualists are compelled to refute statements made from their platforms, because they often invite Theosophist lecturers to speak at Spiritualist meetings. The amusing fact is continually evidenced that, whenever Theosophists want proof of their own statements, they are compelled to refer to mediumistic experiences, though they decry them continually, In the main, the Theosophist adopts yogaistic theories, which credit embodied man with far greater psychic powers than the discarnate spirit.

R. S. Old, who had many years' experience as a Theosophic leader and lecturer, thus sums up their position: '*I have learned all that was to be known about the methods of modern Theosophists. I have weighed them in the balance and found them wanting. They took me from the sunlit hills of spiritual hope and aspiration and led me through shady glens and mysterious paths, through a forest of speculation and doubt, and eventually landed me in a morass of disillusionment from which I was left to extricate myself by an effort of will.*' The poignancy of the summary is fully appreciated by all who gain personal experience of the 'power of the spirit' and go to this body for explanations. They are prolific in theories based upon allegories they misunderstand; but of psychic experience they have none.

The essential difference between the teaching of Allan Kardec and that of other Spiritualists is, first, the practice of 'evocation'; and secondly, the belief in reincarnation.

Evocation means that if you call upon individual spirits with a sincere motive they will respond. The admitted weakness of this idea lies in the fact that auto-suggestion is a very real factor in all mental activities. Next, it was found that personating spirits sometimes answered the call. This the school of Kardec explains by teaching that 'groups of spirits of equal merit adopt certain names and act in the name of the one called upon.' The complications created appear insuperable to Spiritualists, who prefer individualised communications which carry with them the stamp of identity, and who also believe that spontaneous communications are more reliable.

In fairness to all parties, we must remember that subconsciously we automatically invoke certain spirits every time we pray. The sensitive's mind usually relates him to his guide, whose influence he recognises as the channel through which prayer is made effective. The Roman Catholic believes he relates himself to particular saints, and religionists of all schools necessarily indraw the individual spirits who serve the particular religious system they follow. A variation of this idea is adopted by Christians who have given up the belief in a personal Christ and teach that all the great personages of the past were Christs who reincarnated or inspired from the 'Christ' plane. Buddhists would call it the Buddhist plane. In both cases it arises from the wish to extol their god beyond 'other gods'. Old Testament history thus repeats itself.

Allan Kardec's teaching of reincarnation must not be confounded with the speculations of Theosophic or Buddhistic teaching. In particular, Allan Kardec's next world is a very busy practical life, similar in its details to the revelations of Spiritualists the wide world over. It is anything but the abstraction portrayed by the others. It is not a 'waiting' time, but a period of preparation in which the soul consciously prepares for higher developments. Its life of usefulness – according to Kardec – only ceases when the spirit desires to gain additional experience, or perform some expiatory or other work essential to fuller development. He has the privilege of selecting his future father and mother, and it is doubtful consolation to unwise parents to know that they were selected not for their good qualities, but for possibly quite other reasons which might prove advantageous to the child.

Allan Kardec says: 'The doctrine of our freedom in the choice of our successive existences and of the trials which we have to undergo ceases to appear strange when we consider that spirits, being freed from matter, judge of things differently from men. They perceive the ends which these trials are intended to work out – ends far more important to them than the fugitive enjoyments of earth. After each existence they see the steps they have already accomplished, and comprehend what they still lack for the attainment of that purity which alone will enable them to reach the goal; and they willingly submit to the vicissitudes of corporeal life, demanding of their own accord to be allowed to undergo those which will aid them to advance most rapidly. There is, therefore, nothing surprising in a spirit making choice of a hard or painful life. He knows that in his state of imperfection he cannot enjoy the perfect happiness to which he aspires; but he obtains a glimpse of that happiness, and seeks to effect his own improvement, as the sole means of its attainment.'

Because he lived in a Roman Catholic country, though educated in a Protestant one, he accepted the biblical statements with what may be termed a 'modern' explanation, i.e., that which does not appeal to one's common sense, or is historically or scientifically inaccurate, must be read 'symbolically'. The result of this bias is traceable through all his writings. Apostles and biblical characters were frequently evoked and the principal articles are signed with their names. For the rest, I can recommend his *The Spirits' Book* from which some of our extracts are taken, and *The Medium's Book*, as two of the most useful summaries printed concerning Spiritualism or mediumship.

The following story of his birth and unselfish work from boyhood onwards is from Anna Blackwell's translation of 1875: 'Leon Denizarth Hippolyte Rivail, better known by his *nom de plume* of Allan Kardec, was born at Lyons, October 4, 1804 ... Endowed by nature with a passion for teaching, he devoted himself from the age of fourteen to aiding the studies of schoolfellows less advanced than himself. While yet a mere boy, he began to meditate on the means of bringing about a unity of belief among the Christian sects. Having finished his studies at Yverdun, he returned to Lyons in 1824 with the intention of devoting himself to the law; but various acts of religious intolerance to which he unexpectedly found himself subjected led him to renounce the idea ... In 1830 he hired, at his own expense, a large hall in the Rue de Sevres and opened therein courses of gratuitous lectures on chemistry, physics, comparative anatomy and astronomy. He was a member of several learned societies, a voluminous writer of educational works, and a student of mesmerism and phrenology.

'When, about 1850, the phenomenon of table turning was exciting the attention of Europe ... he entered upon a careful investigation of the new phenomena. A friend of his had two daughters who had become what are now called 'mediums'. They were gay, lively, amiable girls, fond of society, dancing and amusement, and habitually received, when 'sitting' by themselves or with their young companions, communications in harmony with their somewhat frivolous dispositions. But, to the surprise of all concerned, it was found that whenever Allan Kardec was present, the messages transmitted through these young ladies were of a very grave and serious character; and on his inquiring of the invisible intelligences as to the cause of this change, he was told that spirits of a much higher order than those who habitually communicated through the two young mediums came expressly for him and would continue to do so, in order to enable him to fulfil an important religious mission. Much astonished at so unlooked-for an announcement, he at once proceeded to test its truthfulness by drawing up a series of progressive questions in relation to the various problems of human life and the universe, receiving their answers through the instrumentality of the two young mediums by table-rapping and planchette writing. The replies have become the basis of the Spiritist theory, which the mediums were as little capable of appreciating as of inventing. Finally, the communicators told him to publish a book under the pseudonym of Allan Kardec and, as indicating that it was the work of spirits rather than his own, he was to call it *Le Livre des Esprits' (The Spirits' Book')*.

Soon after its publication, he founded the Parisian Society of Psychological Studies, of which he was the president until his death on March 31, 1869. The school of Kardec can, therefore, celebrate his birth into the spirit world at the same time as modern Spiritualists celebrate their anniversary.

The general objection to reincarnation is that it is retrogressive and quite out of keeping with nature's usual method of proceeding from a lower to a higher form of manifestation. It also duplicates the starting point of human embodiments. It is obvious that ego number two is superimposed on ego number one unless there is a law whereby one human body possesses an ego while another does not. Spiritualists believe form and soul to be co-existent. Even still-born babies are said to develop to maturity in the spirit world. Some reincarnationists assert that the spirit does not enter the material form until the quickening, or even a later stage. This sets aside the usual belief that all forms of matter are expressions of the divine or creative principle, and that consciousness – termed instinct in the plant and animal – is inherent in the form itself, the only difference between man and the rest of creation being that his spark of divine consciousness becomes individualised and can never afterwards be extinguished. Only the matter of which the physical body is composed returns to its primitive elements. The spiritual counterparts of all forms of life which result from birth in the physical world continue the law of evolution on higher planes of manifestation. Animal consciousness, or instinct, exhibits itself only so long as it is necessary to man's happiness, or its own development on spirit planes.

Alan Kardec thus replies to this aspect: 'All spirits do not think alike in reference to the relations which exist between man and the animals. According to some, spirit only arrives at the human period after having been elaborated and individualised in the different degrees of lower beings of the creation. According to others, the spirit of man has always belonged to the human race, without passing through the ascensional degrees of the animal world. The first of these theories has the advantage of giving an aim to the future of animals, which are thus seen to form the earliest link in the chain of thinking beings. The second theory is more consonant with the dignity of man, and may be summed up as follows: The different species do not proceed intellectually from one another by the road to progression. Thus the spirit of an oyster does not become progressively that of a fish, bird or quadruped, or quadrumane (i.e., four-handed creature like the ape or monkey). Each species is a fixed type, physically and morally, each individual of which draws from the universal source of being, the sum of the intelligent principle which is necessary to it, according to the nature of its organs and the work it has to accomplish in the phenomena of nature, and which it restores to the general mass of that principle at its death…. Man alone possesses the spirit which gives him the moral sense and extended vision.'

The term *Spiritism* is frequently used as a sneer by opponents of Spiritualism who object to classifying it as a religion. The word was originally used by Allan Kardec in precisely the same sense as we use Spiritualism. Kardec used the word *Spiritualism* in a general way to cover all believers in a continued life after death, as Buddhists, Christians, etc. This is actually its correct meaning; but usage more commonly decides the application of words than pedantry. The Roman Catholic hurls *Spiritism* at us as a term of derision, but common use has decided that it denotes 'a believer in spirit manifestations', and is applied to those who admit our facts but refuse to recognise the religion which it inculcates. *Spiritualism* is reserved and applied to those who say; 'The implications of *Spiritism* are religious and the practice of the philosophy derived therefrom is *Spiritualism.*'

I suggest the following lines of thought for your consideration. The majority of Spiritualists oppose the doctrine of reincarnation because they believe the next phase of life contains all the elements essential to progress. The idea of a 'good time' on earth usually relates to physical adjustments rather than spiritual development. The doctrine is often attributable to vanity. Conceit desires glory; so we conjure up dreams of past splendours and quite forget that if we are worse off now than we were, we must have retrogressed and not gone forward. 'Over-shadowing' by a discarnate spirit, or semi-control, produces sensations attributed by many to memory of prior existence. Travelling 'in the spirit' induces similar ideas to the inability of the physical brain to express psychic experiences correctly. Telepathy, prophetic vision and psychometric contact with the past often produce similar ideas.

If it is true that mind moulds matter, reincarnation cannot readjust mentality, it merely complicates the difficulties, and adds to them. The idea is frequently impressed upon sensitives owing to large numbers of believers in reincarnation continually hunting for the next body they believe they must occupy. It thus forms a cause of obsession, but as few people are completely controlled, the dual personality is accepted as part of their prior existence. The great objection to the belief is that it creates an 'earthbound' condition by centring all attention upon physical planes in place of spiritually progressive planes of consciousness.

—⚏—

Note: *The University of Spiritualism* by Harry Boddington was reprinted in 2002 by:

Psychic Press (1995) Ltd
The Coach House
Stansted Hall
Stansted
Essex
CM24 8UD

This book is highly recommended.

CHAPTER 3

Dr. Carl A. Wickland M.D. (1861-1945)

Here we have, without doubt, in my opinion, one of the finest pioneers in medical science, psychiatry and in research for the evidence of survival. Together with his wife Anna, the Wicklands did so much to help humanity.

Carl A. Wickland was born February 14th 1861 at Liden, Norland Province, Sweden. In 1880 he left Sweden and arrived in St.Paul, Minnesota, USA in 1881. He married Anna W. Anderson in 1896 and shortly thereafter they moved to Chicago where Carl Wickland graduated from Durham Medical College in 1900. He studied the general practice of medicine while specialising in research into mental illnesses. This led to Dr. Wickland becoming chief psychiatrist at the National Psychopathic Institute, a non-profit corporation where many patients were treated at the sanatorium and brought back to sanity and health.

Anna Wickland became a very fine sensitive (medium) and worked with her husband to help a great many people whose mental illness was due to obsession by discarnate spirit entities. It was extremely important to bring to the notice of the medical world the truth of the knowledge they had uncovered, and secure medical recognition and acceptance of it.

In 1924 Dr. Wickland, in collaboration with his assistants Nelle Watts, Celia and Orlando Goerz, wrote and published *Thirty Years Among The Dead* which became a classic and was published in five editions in the USA, and had three printings in England and was translated and published in the Netherlands and Spain. Ten years later in 1934 came the first edition of Dr. Wickland's *Gateway Of Understanding*.

Both of these titles take pride of place on my bookshelves and I would certainly recommend my readers to look around for copies of these fine reference works. I mentioned the Wicklands in my previous book *Life Is ForEver* but would like to extend further, by including and quoting some of the important work they were involved with in connection with reincarnation and past lives, and the danger such theories and beliefs held to those attached to them.

Firstly, I should explain how the Wicklands were able to communicate and work with the spirit entities who required help, to release them from the disturbance they were causing to those they were obsessing. Mrs. Wickland being a fine psychic/medium was able to attract the entity into her aura from the patient and from there Dr. Wickland was able to communicate and converse with them. There are so many wonderful examples to read about in these books.

Here is an extract from *Thirty Years Among The Dead* taken from *Chapter XV Theosophy:*

That the belief in reincarnation on earth is a fallacious one and prevents progression to higher spiritual realms after transition has been frequently declared by advanced spirits, while numerous cases of obsession which have come under our care have been due to spirits who, in endeavouring to 'reincarnate' in children, have found themselves imprisoned in the magnetic aura, causing great suffering to both their victims and themselves.

EXPERIENCE, NOVEMBER 19, 1916

Spirit: William Stanley   *Psychic*: Mrs. Wickland

Spirit. Is it really true that I am well now? Can I talk? Can I move my arms and feet? Then reincarnation is true, because before I could neither talk nor walk. How did I get out of the child?

Doctor Wickland.   Intelligent spirits brought you here for help.

Sp. I wanted to come back and reincarnate in a child, and I got in and could not get out. I was so paralyzed that I could not express myself and I was in an awful state.

I was a Theosophist and I wanted to reincarnate to be great. I got into a child's body and crippled it, and also crippled my mind and that of the child. I stayed in the child because I did not know how to get out. I acted as a child and I could not talk.

I know I passed out of my mortal body some years ago, far away in India, but I do not realize when it took place. I wanted so much to reincarnate and to come back to this earth life to live my other karma.

Do not hold on to the thought of coming back, but look for something higher, for the state I was in was the worst torture anybody could have.

I lived in Calcutta and wanted to learn to be a Master and go through my karma, but instead I am as you see me to be.

I reincarnated in a child and became crippled, and I also got into the vibration of the mother. It was very hard and I want to warn others never to come back and try to reincarnate through a little child. Leave reincarnation alone, because it is only a mistake, but the philosophy of Theosophy is very fine.

Look upward; don't think of the astral shells, for they are of no use.

I was very selfish and wanted to come back to earth life just to be something great, but instead I got into a very low state. I had intended to show the Theosophists that I could come back and reincarnate in a child.

Madame Blavatsky should have taught differently *(pointing to an invisible)*. I will tell you, Madame, you are the one who is to blame for the condition I am in today.

Madame Blavatsky stands here trying to help me now. She is the one who gave me the teachings and thoughts of reincarnation, and now she is trying to show me the right way and states there is no such thing as reincarnation.

One gets all mixed up trying to enter another's body for reincarnation.

Dr. What is your name?

Sp. I cannot recall my name just now.

Madame Blavatsky was in India and taught Theosophy. She had many followers and I was with her. I have also met Anna Kingsford and Dr. Hartmann, and he also was to blame for my condition.

They pushed me in here that I might be taught and freed. I am so pleased that I can talk again; that is something I have not been able to do for years.

Madame Blavatsky, Anna Kingsford and the Judge were all great lights, and now they have found out their big mistakes. They are all working to get their victims free, and so they brought me to this place for instruction and guidance.

I was in India, having been there for many years. My father was an officer in the army. I spent most of my time in Calcutta, where I met all the great lights of Theosophy, and I joined the Theosophical Society. I liked Colonel Olcott; he was a great fellow.

I remember being very sick in India for some time. I have no desire to reincarnate again because reincarnation is a wrong doctrine. It creates a selfishness to come back.

I suppose one can learn without being reincarnated. What did I learn in my last reincarnation in the child? What did I learn? I believed in Theosophy and my Karma, and I thought I had to go through with it.

Colonel Olcott belonged to the Great Masters. He belonged to the spirit of Fire and Water – I mean the elementals of Fire and Water

Dr. Have you ever heard of mediums?

Sp. They are only astral shells. Madame Blavatsky says we must all help those who try to reincarnate. She and the others have come to say they are trying to help and for that purpose have formed a big society.

I thought I had come to life when I came here, and that I could reincarnate and to talk to them as I did in life. I did not know they had passed over. Teaching as they did, why did they not reincarnate the same as I?

Madame Blavatsky was a great missionary, as you know. She says she is now trying to make all her victims understand about the life after this as it really is.

She says that she was a medium at one time, but that she did not want anybody to control her. She thought you should develop your own self and mental faculties, and go through your Karma.

I should not have been taught the falseness I was. Madame tells me that I should listen to this gentleman (Dr. W.) and that he will explain things.

Explanations were given regarding life on the earth plane, the preparation for the life that is to follow, and the fact that the knowledge and wisdom gained here will be the light of understanding each one carries to the other side of life.

The spirit finally gave the name of William Stanley, and departed, grateful for the enlightenment he had received.

—⚡—

I will now quote from *The Gateway of Understanding Chapter XI Reincarnation and* Theosophy:

Long years of contact with the Invisible World and the lessons obtained from dwellers in that school of life cause the doctrine of reincarnation to lose its plausibility. Any foundation for belief in this theory receives a better interpretation when we understand the influence and thought waves emanating from discarnate spirits which act upon a sensitive brain much as sound waves are conveyed through the radio, a fact equally demonstrated through Psychic Research, especially the abnormal phase.

The theory of reincarnation can undoubtably be traced to early stages of mankind when departed spirits took possession of the bodies of sensitive individuals and lived and acted through them, thus seemingly indicating reincarnation. But in reality this was only spirit obsession or possession.

Swedenborg states in *Heaven and its Wonders and Hell*:

There is such conjunction between the spiritual world and the natural world in man that the two are seemingly one ... (It is) provided that there should be angels and spirits with each individual... .

With every individual there are good spirits and evil spirits ... by the two he is kept in equilibrium, and being in equilibrium he is in freedom... .

Good and evil are two opposites ... Unless man were between these two he could have no thought nor any will, still less any freedom or any choice, for all these man has by virtue of the equilibrium between good and evil... .

Every man in respect to his spirit, even while he is living in the body, is in some society with spirits although he does not know it ...

If a spirit were to speak from his own memory with a man, the man would not know otherwise than that the thoughts then in his mind were his own, although they were the spirit's thoughts. This would be like the recollection of something which the man had never heard or seen.

This is the source of the belief held by some of the ancients that after some thousands of years they were to return into their former life, or had returned. This they concluded because at times there came to them a sort of recollection of things they had never seen or heard. This came from an influx from the memory of spirits into their ideas of thought.

Such occurrences are not limited to primitive races but obtain today in the possession by selfish or ignorant spirits of sensitive persons whose identity becomes entirely changed by these various forms of encroachment; but today this is designated as mental aberration or insanity.

The supposed 'memories' of past lives of those who believe in reincarnation are far better accounted for by the presence of invisible intelligences whose memories of their own mortal careers are conveyed through thought waves to the reincarnationists who have become sensitized to such impressions by their meditations and negativism.

Mischievous entities who enjoy playing pranks can also impress upon sensitive minds all sorts of false 'memories' which please the victim's vanity.

A woman who was a Theosophist stated to us, as proof of reincarnation, that whenever she read ancient history she invariably remembered the events about which she was reading, not realizing that interfering spirits were producing those mental pictures.

Is it not curious that the 'memories' of past lives which 'recur' to these believers in the theory of reincarnation are essentially concerned with wonderful careers of greatness in the past, they usually recalling themselves only as kings, Cleopatras, Apostles, Great Patriachs, etc.?

Annie Besant believed herself to be the reincarnation of Hypatia and Giordano Bruno, and a report from England states there are at least fifty presumed Cleopatras in that country today. Individuals holding such beliefs are not real analysts but mere sentimentalists;

they mistake the impressions of discarnated spirits for memories of their own past lives.

If reincarnation had been a fact through the ages should we not find evidence of it in a goodly portion of superior human beings who had advanced to a high degree of knowledge and development? But there is no evidence of such supermen; only a general average is noticeable among mankind.

Were the theory true that re-birth is required for attaining perfection, should there not be more evidence of perfected souls among us than is discernible – aside from the number of self-hypnotized individuals who imagine themselves to have attained that goal?

During our years of Psychic Research we have contacted many discarnated spirits of various conditions who said they had been seeking for a chance to reincarnate but with the only result of becoming lodged in the aura of some person sensitive to spirit encroachment, thereby causing great distress to the victim of such obsession.

Often such entities inspire bizarre notions and hallucinations in the victim's mind, yet the individual may be unaware that a spirit is causing the delusions and the entity may be unaware of being a spirit or of interfering with anyone, and both may be skeptical regarding spirit influence.

Instead of being helpful, the doctrine of reincarnation is very pernicious, since earthly-minded individuals with strong attractions to the physical world, may learn of the theory of rebirth and fix firmly in their minds the determination to reincarnate again, hoping to obtain a better opportunity to carry out their earthly propensities. We have contacted many such spirits who were firm believers in reincarnation yet were unaware of being so-called dead; often in their ignorance they claimed to be wonderful 'Masters', and yet they were only earthbound spirits. A great deal of reasoning was required to disillusion them, cause them to realize their situation and open their mental eyes to the road of spiritual progression.

Several children with mental aberrations, who came under our care, proved to be influenced by spirits who had attempted to reincarnate and found themselves enmeshed in the auras of the children, thus interfering with the children's normal physical and mental development as well as hindering their own spiritual progression.

The spirit of Madame Blavatsky, speaking through Mrs. Wickland, said of the theory of reincarnation:

I see now that my teachings caused many to become psychic sensitives and that the theory of reincarnation causes much obsession. I also taught that one should be a vegetarian, but the majority live under too great a nervous tension for this and become too sensitive.

I have found that 'reincarnation' is possible only through obsession, and I have also found, to my great sorrow, that many of my followers become obsessed.

It is dangerous to teach the theory of reincarnation because many selfish people, who come to the other side of life, look for what they consider the right place to reincarnate but they do not understand obsession and therefore disturb and obsess children. That is one reason there are so many idiot children in the asylums.

I was a psychic when in earth life and I knew spirits could come back and control mortals. I realize now that if I had taught the philosophy of Theosophy and the truth of spirit return it would have been much better.

We cannot progress to the higher life of understanding with a falsehood on our minds; an understanding of the truth is necessary.

World travellers, missionaries authors and lecturers alike bear testimony that in India, where belief in reincarnation is general, cases of obsession and possession are exceedingly prevalent.

Reincarnation is also a convenient excuse for selfishness since those with wealth and those born in more favourable circumstances may credit their own position to many incarnations and attainment through rebirths and assume they are now enjoying their just dues because of their 'good Karma'; while the lowly and unfortunate ones who, because they were born in unfavourable conditions and raised in squalor and poverty, have been deprived of the better opportunities of life, are regarded as supposed victims of their own 'bad Karma'.

To hold that the inequalities and miseries in this world are due to wrong acts, or acts of omission and commission in former lives which have established an unbalance necessitating reincarnation in order to work out the supposed 'Karmic Law of Justice', merely condones the selfishness so prevalent in the world and the self-aggrandizement of the few which deprives the many of proper opportunity to realise the purpose of existence.

Selfishness and ignorance have blinded humanity to the purpose of the Creator; the idea that self-preservation is the first law in nature has prevailed from the dawn of existence to the present time. This has been the source of much evil and wrong all through the ages, as well as the cause of untold oppression by the worldly mighty and of untold misery to the less fortunate, who have been held down by unreasonable creeds, cults and dogmas, and deprived of all opportunity to gain any intelligent understanding of the meaning of their existence.

The theory of reincarnation subverts the natural spiritual progression; too much stress and importance is placed upon this brief mortal life. The teaching of the reincarnationists that we must return again and again to earth life to become perfected is equivalent to saying that, one has passed through kindergarten, grade schools and university, he must return to kindergarten over and over again to learn everything that is to be learned pertaining to life.

What is mortal life but a kindergarten? Too little is credited to the vaster opportunities of the next school in the spiritual realm, the verity of which has been so abundantly demonstrated and which may be easily verified by the unprejudiced student through intelligent Psychic Research.

The entire scheme of reincarnation is a limited idea, one that fails to recognise this is a formative plane and that there are many planes and schools on the Invisible Side which offer far greater opportunities for the higher soul culture than does this mortal plane. There is no need of returning to the mundane when we can progress from sphere to sphere, or school to school, and thus ultimately realize the 'God within'.

To live morally and uprightly, to learn in this life what we are living for, and to realize there are future opportunities, is undoubtably the cardinal object of our human existence.

The Spirit of Rudolph Valentino, communicating through Mrs. Wickland, spoke at length of the reincarnation theory and of conditions as they actually are in the spirit world. The question was put to him: *Do you still believe in reincarnation?*

'I have found matters to be very different in that respect from what I thought. Reincarnation, as it is generally understood, is not necessary. A spirit that realizes his condition and understands progression is not interested in reincarnation; to reincarnate in a physical body on this earth again would be very foolish.

But very few spirits seek for the spirit world when they pass out. Some spirits who have gone beyond the veil of death are in the dark, some are in semi-darkness, some are in twilight, some in the light.

The ones who have found the light are those who understand, who have knowledge of life in spirit; these would never think of coming back to earth again in a physical body.

They come back as spirits, to be invisible teachers, to guide and help humanity. This might be called a 'reincarnation of the soul' but without physical birth; it is only a temporary measure. It is not reincarnation in the flesh, but in spirit, to help and serve. They can come back to their dear ones and help them in many ways when they know the laws.

But many spirits are ignorant of their true situation and very few seek for the spirit world when they pass out. Ignorance is darkness and they have to be awakened to see the light.

Intelligent spirits enlighten and teach these ignorant ones, often taking them to earth to contact material things; in this way many souls are brought to earth to acquire earth experience with the help of enlightened spirits. Through matter they awaken and see and learn through different experiences.

We may say this is reincarnating to earth life in soul, but not in a physical body. They are brought to earth as spirits to correct their mistakes. In that way they can be of help to those they have wronged by serving, protecting and guarding them. That is their mission.

They must do good for any wrong committed; they cannot progress until they have served in one way or another the ones they have injured. No matter how small the misdeed, the wrong must be replaced by good.

That is justice; the scales of justice must balance. After spirits have done their duty they are taken to other spheres to learn lessons which lead to progression.

Is this not much better than to reincarnate as a child? A spirit who believed in reincarnation on earth wakens from the sleep into which he has hypnotized himself and thinks it is time for him to reincarnate. He hopes to come in contact with the birth of some child; sometimes he succeeds in doing this – but what has actually happened?

He has possessed that child and that is a sin. These facts should be taught during earth life; people will then understand and be so much happier.'

In *Illuminated Brahmanism* a communication transmitted by the spirit Ranga Hilyod, the ancient Indian teacher called the Great Brahma, an explanation is given of the original Brahminical doctrines '……. and the perversion of a great truth into a malign superstition …. which has become a source of the most pestilent spiritual mischief.

There is one effect of the doctrine of reincarnation of the souls of the dead that is felt with direful power in the spiritual world of India. Myriads who have left the physical life hover over the mortals of that country seeking for opportunities to become re-embodied, in order that they may realize the promised relief from their imperfect development in the former earth life. They are earthbound to a degree that infects the mental atmosphere of its people with almost hopeless despair, for however intense may be their desire, they are never able to obtain the fancied reincarnation.

Could India emancipate herself from the tyranny of the idea of reincarnation, she would rise in the scale of spiritual enlightenment far higher than she rose in the age of the Vedas or when Capilya or Gautama led her hosts toward the heavenly paradise. She must do this or she must remain the prey to vile superstitions, and her moral nature be degraded by the mental influx of myriad hosts who strive in vain to realize the truth of the dogma.

I taught that one God alone was Supreme, and the true object of adoration and praise. I taught that from this Being all who passed from physical life would return, but I never taught that returning to the presence spiritual of the great Om would result in the annihilation of the individual or his inability to return to earth as a spirit.

I did teach that all spirits could return to earth to manifest, and influence mortals, and I also taught that such a return would be determined by the mental bias of the individual.

There were those who could not understand how a spirit could come to earth without being re-embodied in physical life ... To suppose that in the statements which I left on record as to the nature of the soul there is or ever was any basis for the present theory of transmigration, is to pervert a great truth until it has become a most grievous error. I taught that the pathway of the race was upward, not downward, and that the world of spirit held in itself the power to emancipate all souls from the thralldom of spiritual slavery.

Whenever any great soul arises from earth, manifesting the attributes of wisdom and love, such a soul does not lose its power of expression upon earth, for there will ever be correlative spirits born there through which the higher developed mind in spirit can give expression to its own existence ... As individuals they can only return through the power of the spiritual transfer of thought, which enables them to register upon the mentality of mortals the wisdom that pertains to the world of developed mind.

The law of spiritual unfoldment is this, that the better the conditions the wiser and purer the life; and while it may be necessary for the spiritual entity to lay its foundation in planetary life, the sooner it can escape from bad conditions there the more likely it will be to have a beautiful development. It may have to stay in the mortal environment for a season to perfect the form powers, but when that is once accomplished no necessity exists for further imprisonment upon earth, for all that earth can teach is what pertains to the physical senses rather than to the spiritual life, and to condemn a spirit to return to it after once having had its nature developed in that direction would be to degrade rather than exalt the soul, nor could anything be gained by it.

By the law of spiritual evolution, the spirit once having had its formative stages in earthly or planetary life has no more necessity for returning to that condition than the developed bird has to re-enter the shell of the embryonic period.

The law does not call for the return to the environment of earth after its escape from the atmosphere of earthly thoughts, nor does it ever need to express itself again in the realm of earthly embodiment. Its pathway to Nirvana is away from earth, and happy the soul who is freed from the idea of ever having to tread the path through mortal life again.'

The communication, *Illuminated Buddhism,* purported to have been psychically received from the spirit Siddartha Sakya Muni, presents the following views of reincarnation:

'When the error went forth from what was considered competent authority, through the Brahmin priesthood, that metempsychosis was the destiny of the spirit, the mentality of India was so poisoned by it that for centuries there was no improvement or desire for relief except in annihilation.

The myriad victims (of this error) have been seeking the relief from consequences that result from the notations of the natural law of spirit unfoldment and have crowded back to the earth, seeking in vain to become reincarnated over and over again, hoping against hope for generations ... By inductive transfer of thought (these spirits) have infected the mental world of the mortals of India with a hopeless despair … and the nation has sunk under the burden of this weight of ignorance.

The only incarnation that will give relief is the embodiment of spiritual light upon a basis of scientific demonstration, and the only metempsychosis that will avail its people is the lifting of the soul from the belief or desire of any further experience in the world of physical life to the infinite unfoldment that awaits the spirit in the worlds immortal. It is there that the true metempsychosis is to be experienced.

Developed spirits who have attained the states of freedom from desire and the disposition of benevolence do not wish to ever return to the atmosphere of earth, but on the part of those who are ignorant devotees of transmigration there is a great tendency to cling to earth. The hope of reincarnation is entirely vain and serves no good purpose, but retards the spirit from going forward in the spheres of unfolding thought. When the spirit is freed from its earthly form it should be able to go onward in the spheres of eternal unfoldment.'

We need to realize that this mundane existence is but a primary school for the unfoldment of consciousness and other innate mental faculties and that at "death" the spirit, freed from physical cares and hindrances, enters the next school where greater opportunities are available for progressive attainment and understanding of God's Plan.

If mankind will set aside prejudice and, in place of the dogmatic cults and isms which, aside from any moral precepts they may contain, are in so many instances only opiates to the soul, open-mindedly co-operate with the

Intelligences from the next school of life, who are ever eager to convey the assurance that they are not 'dead', it will revolutionize the world's conception of the Creator and the creation of which we are a part and afford an intelligent understanding of the meaning of life, the lack of which is keeping the world in doubt and despair.

When this inter-communication is fully established then. and then only, will humanity begin to discern the fundamental wrongs of the prevailing system of economies which have hitherto not been fully comprehended. It will reveal that the education and enlightenment of the soul, as it passes through this mundane sphere, is a primary object and that experiences pertaining to the physical life are only a means for that accomplishment.

The advancement of science and research and the inventions for human betterment are gradually bringing about the dawn of a new era and, in spite of opposition, are replacing dogmas and useless creeds with enlightenment and knowledge.

In lieu of accepting dogmas, reincarnation theories or other beliefs let humanity waken to the fact that the teachings of the Nazarene have a scientific background, that all mankind is bound together and no man can live unto himself alone. Everyone born into this life should have the fullest opportunity for soul culture.

Change the economic system; let ideal educational opportunities be provided and each individual, from early infancy, have the proper surroundings where the best possible physical and mental environment are afforded; let the latent finer sensibilities be evolved through loving kindness and quickened through object lessons – music, arts, sciences and the beautiful in nature.

If such ideal conditions could obtain through a few generations the average of human intelligences would be so far advanced that dogmas and creeds, as well as the idea of reincarnation, would be as obsolete as the gods of mythology. Onward and upward is the trend of evolution – from the darkness of ignorance to the light of understanding. This is clearly Nature's Plan.

CHAPTER 4

Reports and Quotes

Past and Present

Of the apparent split in France between Kardec's beliefs in reincarnation and those of M. Pierart, publisher of the opposition journal, *Le Revue Spiritualiste*, the *London Spiritual Magazine* sought to comment in 1865:

To this doctrine – which has nothing to do with Spiritualism, even if it had a leg of reason or fact to stand on – all the strength, and almost all the space of these journals is devoted.

These are the things which give the enemies of spiritualism a real handle against it, and bring it into contempt with sober minds. Reincarnation is a doctrine which cuts up by the roots all individual identity in the future existence. It desolates utterly that dearest yearning of the human heart for reunion with its loved ones in a permanent world. If some are to go back into fresh physical bodies, and bear new names, and new natures, if they are to become respectively Tom Styles, Ned Snooks, and a score of other people, who shall ever hope to meet again with his friends, wife, children, brothers and sisters? When he enters the spirit world and enquires for them, he will have to learn that they are already gone back to earth, and are somebody else, the sons and daughters of other people, and will have to become over and over the kindred of a dozen other families in succession! Surely, no such most cheerless crochet could bewitch the intellects of any people, except the most especial bedevilment of the most sarcastic and mischievous of devils.

The following extracts referring to Allan Kardec and Spiritism and the stance taken by Spiritualism are taken from *The History of Spiritualism Vol. Two* by Sir Arthur Conan Doyle:

Kardec considered that the words 'spiritual', 'spiritualist', and 'spiritualism' already had a definite meaning. Therefore he substituted 'spiritism' and 'spiritist'.

This Spiritist philosophy is distinguished by its belief that our spiritual progression is effected through a series of incarnations.

Kardec conducted his investigations through the communicating intelligences by means of question and answer, and in this way obtained the material for his books............

Spiritualists in England have come to no decision with regard to reincarnation. Some believe in it, many do not, and the general attitude may be taken to be that, as the doctrine cannot be proved, it had better be omitted from the active politics of Spiritualism. Miss Anna Blackwell, in explanation of this attitude, suggests that the continental mind being more receptive of theories, has accepted Allan Kardec, while the English mind 'usually declines to consider any theory until it has assured itself of the facts assumed by such theory.'

Mr. Thomas Brevior (Shorter), one of the editors of *THE SPIRITUAL MAGAZINE*, sums up the prevailing view of English Spiritualists of his day. He writes:

THE SPIRITUAL MAGAZINE, 1876, p. 35.

When Reincarnation assumes a more scientific aspect, when it can offer a body of demonstrable facts admitting of verification like those of Modern Spiritualism, it will merit ample and careful discussion. Meanwhile, let the architects of speculation amuse themselves if they will by building castles in the air; life is too short, and there is too much to do in this busy world to leave either leisure or inclination to occupy ourselves in demolishing these airy structures, or in showing on what slight foundations they are reared. It is far better to work out those points in which we are agreed than to wrangle over those upon which we appear so hopelessly to differ.

William Howitt, one of the stalwarts of early Spiritualism in England, is still more emphatic in his condemnation of reincarnation. After quoting Emma Hardinge Britten's remark that *thousands in the Other World protest, through distinguished mediums, that they have no knowledge or proofs of reincarnation*, he says (p.57):

The thing strikes at the root of all faith in the revelations of Spiritualism. If we are brought to doubt the spirits communicating under the most serious guise, under the most serious affirmations, where is Spiritualism itself? If Reincarnation be true, pitiable and repellent as it is, there must have been millions of spirits who, on entering the other world, have sought in vain their kindred, children and friends. Has even a whisper of such a woe ever reached us from the thousands and tens of thousands of communicating spirits? Never.

We may, therefore, on this ground alone, pronounce the dogma of Reincarnation false as the hell from which it sprung.

The Hon. Alexander Aksakof, in an interesting article *The Spiritualist Vol. VII (1875) pp 74-75* supplies the names of the mediums at Allan Kardec's circle, with an account of them. He also points out that a belief in the idea of reincarnation was strongly held in France at that time, as can be seen from M. Pezzani's work, *The Plurality of Existences*, and others. Aksakof writes:

That the propagation of this doctrine by Kardec was a matter of strong predilection is clear; from the beginning Reincarnation has not been presented as an object of study, but as a dogma. To sustain it he has always had recourse to writing mediums, who, it is well known, pass so easily under the psychological influence of preconceived ideas; and Spiritism has engendered such in profusion; whereas through physical mediums the communications are not only more objective, but always contrary to the doctrine of Reincarnation. Kardec adopted the plan of always disparaging this kind of mediumship, alleging as a pretext its moral inferiority. Thus the experimental method is altogether unknown in Spiritism; for twenty years it has not made the slightest intrinsic progress, and it has remained in total ignorance of Anglo-American Spiritualism! The few French physical mediums who developed their powers in spite of Kardec, were never mentioned by him in the 'Revue'; they remained almost unknown to Spiritists, and only because their spirits did not support the doctrine of Reincarnation.

D. D. Home, in commenting on Aksakof's article, has a thrust at a phase of the belief in reincarnation. He says:

THE SPIRITUALIST, Vol. VII., p. 165.
I meet many who are reincarnationists, and I have had the pleasure of meeting at least twelve who were Marie Antoinette, six or seven Mary Queen of Scots, a whole host of Louis and other kings, about twenty Alexander the Greats, but it remains for me yet to meet a plain John Smith, and I beg of you, if you meet one, to cage him as a curiosity.

—◊—

The respected medium Robin Stevens was a regular contributor to *Psychic News* answering readers questions. The following is Robin's answer to a question appearing in *Psychic News* dated 6th March 1993:

Question: *Eastern religion strongly pushes the view that each human soul reincarnates and there appears to be fairly good evidence to suggest this.*
What is the possibility of never having the chance to meet loved ones who have passed on because they have reincarnated to resume their karma before one's own transition to the spirit world?

Answer: Dear M.R., Scotland. The concept of reincarnation as a part of Spiritualist belief is, to me, totally incongruous.
History shows that Western culture was influenced by the Theosophical movement at the same time as the emergence of modern Spiritualism.

One prime exponent of Theosophic principles was Madame Blavatsky. Her revelations were in reality no more than a mixture of Buddhistic, Brahmanistic and Kabalistic matter.

The conflict between Spiritualism and reincarnation centres around the acceptance of a continuous, eternal evolution of the soul and the seeming necessity to return to the physical and material world in order to progress.

The strength of Spiritualist philosophy rests in the exercise of free will. If the desire for reuniting with loved ones is a common wish, it will be so.

It has also been suggested to me that the opportunity must exist to make good our faults and equally to reap our rewards, particularly in the next state of existence. As this seems to suggest reconciliation with loved ones is an essential part of that process, your concern is unfounded.

—〰—

Rev. Charles L. Tweedale, Vicar of Weston, Otley, W. Yorkshire. Another fine pioneer and researcher. He wrote a number of books of which I am fortunate enough to have copies in my home library of two famous works; *Man's Survival After Death* (second edition 1920) and *News From The Next World* (second edition 1940). There is a wealth of information in these books covering such a vast amount of psychic happenings and mediumship of all kinds experienced and witnessed by Charles Tweedale together with his family, friends and colleagues.

It is with regard to reincarnation that I wish to quote for this, my book. With all the experience Tweedale had of the paranormal, survival and the afterlife, I can find nothing to support reincarnation or past lives from the two great works I have in my possession and which together run into nearly one thousand pages.

On page 347 of *News From The Next World* Charles Tweedale states:

Proof of survival after death we have in abundance, but absolutely no proof of reincarnation as a general principle. Such proof if it were obtainable would be <u>the greatest calamity that ever befell mankind</u>, for at one stroke it would sweep away the continuity of human individuality, destroy the anticipation of meeting and recognising loved ones in the future life, reduce survival to a farce and human existence to a travesty.

If reincarnation were really true as a general principle and experience, then <u>who would any man really be</u>? Would he be John Smith, Julius Caesar or Nebuchadnezzar. Who would any woman be? Who would any woman's child be? The height of absurdity is reached when it is alleged that in this reincarnation, the <u>sex</u> also may be changed, and that a man may be the reincarnation of his great-great-great- … grandmother who lived under a different nationality thousands of years ago!! In fact there is no limit to the absurdities and inconsistencies of this most pernicious and reprehensible reincarnation theory, which strikes at the root of that survival of <u>conscious individuality</u> which alone can bring any satisfaction to the mind.

On page 343 of the same volume a Naval Officer stated:

There is no reincarnation. When I rowed my boat over here I did not leave my oars crossed.

The S.N.U. (Spiritualists National Union) does not accept the theory of reincarnation. In the Lyceum

Manual (lesson No: 136) on the teachings of Spiritualism it states:

Concerning all spiritual Life, State and Being, Spiritualism accepts no theories that are not sustained by proven facts and corroborative testimony.

Ken Beetham (SNU Diploma holder and healer) has written much and spoken out against what he calls the 'New-Age rubbish' and the following of pseudo science by so many today rather than keeping in line with the science and philosophy laid down by those fine pioneers.

The following articles by Ken Beetham are taken from his book *Just Thoughts:*

REINCARNATION?

Emma Hardinge Britten was completely against the idea of reincarnation and once stated that '*It owed more to the imagination than it did to reason.*'

In his studies on the human psyche Carl Gustav Jung stated that '*When reason and imagination are in conflict, imagination will always win.*' The Spiritualists National Union states that '*As there is no evidence of reincarnation that can not be explained by other means, it is therefore not part of the religion of Spiritualism.*'

So let us put imagination to one side and examine the facts as we know them. It appears that the apparent remembrance of previous lives can all be answered by four known facts:

Fact 1. The human brain is capable of storing an incredible amount of facts. Every sensory impression, everything ever heard, even conversations heard as a baby of a few months old, everything ever read is stored in the depths of the unconscious mind.

These memories very rarely surface into the conscious mind until they are stimulated by electrical impulses to the brain or by hypnosis. This process is known by the name <u>Cryptomnesia.</u>

Fact 2. In his studies of the mind, Jung stated that every human molecule had within it a memory of all that had ever happened to, not just the person, but to all his family and ancestors stretching way back into the mists of time. He called this the <u>Ancestral Memory</u>. In this age of enlightenment we would call this <u>Genetic Memory</u>. It will be interesting to see that when they finally clone the first human whether the clone retains this memory, although Dolly the sheep seems to have retained all the sheep memories and habits of its parent.

Fact 3. As Spiritualists we are aware of the proven fact of overshadowing, in fact we are so used to it that sometimes we are inclined to forget it is happening.

The Welsh hypnotherapist Arnall Bloxham, a great believer in reincarnation, was one of the first men to attempt regression into past lives and his book *The Bloxham Tapes* became a best seller and started a trend which has gathered pace and still continues. The famous case of the York Jewess killed in the Jewish massacre of 1190 was so convincing that people took it as proof that reincarnation was a fact. Unfortunately a researcher named Melvin Harris spent many months researching the evidence and found that most of the story relied upon modern misconceptions and not on historical fact.

Following up on this he researched another previous life of the same lady, a Roman woman named Livonia and found all the characters and plots in two novels by Louis de Wohl, books which the woman had no recollection of ever reading.

Result — **Cryptomnesia.**

It is interesting however to learn as more evidence of cryptomnesia was brought forward, Bloxham found that if he tried to regress patients without their knowledge he could not do so, and he gave up the practice. Before his death in the eighties he stated that he now doubted any of his regressions were into past lives, but had other explanations of which cryptomnesia was only one. He also stated that in some cases, he suspected that some form of 'spiritual phenomena' could be at work.

Professor Ian Stevenson has been researching past lives for over forty years and has produced many papers on the subject in which he cautiously suggests may be proof of other lives. He completely rules out regression hypnosis but has based his 'proofs' on spontaneous recall. Unfortunately for him he hasn't had the advantage of a Spiritualist education, and the spontaneous recall he relies so much upon can be easily explained by overshadowing (I myself am a good example of this). He did however check hundreds of reports from India and Asia of young children claiming previous lives, and he found out that in almost every case the child claimed a higher and therefore richer family, and usually one within a few miles of his own home.

Writer and researcher Ian Wilson also studied the reincarnation children of India and noted that the children always claimed a higher caste and that this might indicate the presence of another motive of perceived financial awards. So it seems we have found another fact – fraud!

KARMA

This dangerous fallacy that disability or ill health is a deserved lesson to be learned, must be taken to its ultimate effect to be fully understood.

Much of the increase in present day illness, cancer etc. is undoubtedly due to use of chemical food additives, air and water pollution by artificial fertilisation of the land, radiation and the constant search for a magic and very lucrative pill.

As a healer I understand that regardless of the diversity of the cause, the healing process is always the same. Love and the ability to attune to the Healing Spirit.

Although the belief in karma has been sanitised in the Western world for the consumption of New-Age enthusiasts, its basic premises cannot be glossed over.

Its precepts are based upon the ignorant belief of a vengeful, vindictive, punishing God, or Gods as the case may be. A belief which to a modern scientifically based religion like Spiritualism is an affront to the Great Spirit.

Mother Theresa of Calcutta spent most of her life fighting the ultimate result of this belief.

Sick and starving children and adults are left dying in the streets by people who could easily help them, simply because it is their karma to suffer and die this way. This belief is so ingrained into their religious teachings that they walk past these karmic victims very carefully in case their shadows fall upon these poor souls, thus giving them a few seconds relief from the heat of the sun. For this would be a sin against one of the many gods they worship.

It was used by power seeking politicians and so called holy men for their own purposes and in India was the main reason for the rise of the evil caste system.

Nehru who was a complete agnostic was so fed up with the many gods and holy men who fed off his countrymen like a plague of locusts (his words) that he threatened them with dire consequences if they didn't get their act together and join their many gods and sacred books and incompatible philosophies into a single *all India* system.

Thus the *all India* religion of Modern Hinduism was born and must not be confused with the older version which evolved from Brahmanism. It is an invented one and does not spring from any one source – unless you count political expediency e.g. the Upishads were far removed from other religious practices, yet the rituals of floridly painted images, caste, bathing in ashes, pilgrimages and fasting, have all been embraced by the so called *all India* religion.

The doctrines of rebirth and karma (the working out of ones actions committed in other lives) were still affirmed, but thankfully in these modern times are being seriously questioned.

Indian religious thinkers are realising that this belief does not make sense when attempts are made to blend it with modern biology and genetics. Even the uneducated among them are asking ; 'If I owe my characteristics to two parents there must be no place for a third force (the effects of my previous actions). Therefore it can only follow that previous actions cannot exist.'

It seems that in modern India under the *all India* religion, there are now very few problems in believing in a one God system. However serious doubts are now emerging about Reincarnation and Karma.

Unfortunately the writer Aldous Huxley popularised this belief in the Western world and other people including so called religious gurus saw the chance of book sales, seminars, regressions, past-life therapy and like poor Topsy it just grew and grew and grew.

Two of the propagators of the Eastern doctrine of karma were the founder of Theosophy, Madame Blavatsky who spent her childhood in a home saturated in superstition, imagination and fantasy, and her disciple Annie Besant. To attempt to understand these mixed up ladies would take several books, and many have been written. A report on Blavatsky by the American Society for Psychical Research however, stated that she was one of the most accomplished, ingenious and most interesting impostors in history.

In an Eastern programme on TV a few months ago the top actress in Indian cinema was asked what made her become an actress? She replied that the only way to make a good living in India was to be either a politician, a holy man or an actress. The last category was her only choice, and remember she is living in modern atom bomb owning India.

As I see it, man-made religions from the ancient world down through the ages to the New-Age movements, have misunderstood the true meaning of karma and how it works. Karma is not punishment or reward. It simply means that you will sow what you reap, and like is certain to attract like. It is an immutable Spiritual Law which rationally means that if you send out negative thoughts then you will attract the negative thoughts of others, and vice versa. Taken to its logical conclusion this means that by our thoughts, which of course control our actions, <u>we create our own reality</u>, regardless of which part of our spiritual journey we happen to be experiencing.

It has nothing to do with an enraged, vengeful God, venting his spleen on his terrified creation. I will repeat the words of the famous spirit-guide Tine Seine Tie, who, through the trance mediumship of J.J.Morse – a former editor of *Two Worlds* – stated:

Reincarnation is a question that has taken hold of the imagination of people rather than their intellects. All other faculties have either been subordinated or entirely dulled in relation to the consideration involved. In all cases there is not the slightest warrant in the laws of nature, the principles of being, or the constitution of man to give the slightest foundation for the reality of these assertions.

He then stressed the evil implications of the belief in karma:

If you are brought back into this world as a consequence of your past-life because you have accumulated a karma that must be outworked in the world in which that karma originated, then, if that law holds good it follows that you have no right to alleviate the wretchedness of men.

After more observations from the guide, he finishes with these words:

Reincarnation is an intellectual monstrosity, a philosophical absurdity, and spiritually untrue. We speak knowingly.

—m—

Emma Hardinge Britten (1823-1899)

I have quoted this great pioneer and outstanding medium a number of times throughout this book. Perhaps the most renowned and respected advocate and proponent of the early Spiritualist Movement, and for spreading the certain evidence of survival.

She was the daughter of Captain Floyd Hardinge, whom writers call a seafaring man. Early in her life, she had shown gifts as a musician, singer and speaker. In fact, at the age of 11 she was earning her living as a music teacher.

Under contract with a theatrical company, she went to America in 1856 where, through the mediumship of Miss Ada Hoyt (Mrs. Coan), she became converted to the Spiritualist philosophy. There, she began developing her own abilities as a medium and sat publicly for the *Society for the Diffusion of Spiritual Knowledge of New York.*

As a young medium, she furnished one of the best attested cases of early Spirit return. A member of the crew of the mail steamer, 'Pacific', which had sunk in the ocean, controlled young Emma and, in trance, disclosed the facts of the tragedy. Because of the nature of the details given through her mediumship, Emma Hardinge was threatened with prosecution by the owners of the boat when the story was made public, but all the details were found to be true and accurate.

Her mediumistic gifts embraced automatic writing, psychometry, healing, prophesy and inspirational speaking. She was best known for her addresses, which were very eloquent, inspired and informative. They were given completely extempore, and the subject was generally chosen in the auditorium by a committee from the audience.

Most historians agree that, as a propagandist for Spiritualism, she was unequaled in her zeal, commitment and enthusiasm. For years she travelled all over the United States, Canada, England, Australia and New Zealand, expounding the truths of Spiritualism and related areas of thought.

Emma Hardinge Britten founded and edited, for five years, the *Two Worlds* of Manchester. She was also among the founders of the *Theosophical Society* in New York in 1875. However, she soon severed her connections with Madame Blavatsky.

Although she had since passed on (1899), her dream of establishing a proper and formal training school for mediums was realised in 1900 with the founding of the *Britten Memorial Institute and Library* in Manchester, England.

Emma Hardinge Britten's writings include:

Modern American Spiritualism (New York 1870); *Nineteenth Century Miracles* (New York 1884); *Faith, Fact and Fraud of Religious History* (Manchester 1896); Extemporaneous *Addresses* (London 1866). She was editor of the American periodical, *The Western Star* (1872) and the British *The Unseen Universe* (1892-1893).

Her classic *Modern American Spiritualism* is still considered the finest and most complete analysis of the early American Movement. We remember her as a true pioneer and dedicated advocate of Spiritualism.

As editor of *The Unseen Universe* Emma Hardinge Britten was asked for her reasons for rejecting the doctrine of reincarnation and its relation to Spiritualism?

She said she rejected the doctrine because it was totally unproved. She added:

Much as I loathe the thought or bare possibility of living again as a mortal on this cold, hard, sorrowful world, I would willingly bend my mind acceptance of the idea, were it capable of proof or demonstration.

She went on to quote Swedenborg who despite his year of intercourse with *Teaching Angels* and his travels through the spheres, totally denied any assumption of a return to earth.

The followers of Mesmer and especially the French clairvoyants, also denied even its possibility. She pointed out that in American Spiritualism, reincarnation was not only not taught, but to questioners on the subject, emphatically rejected.

Emma added:

The doctrine of a return to earth for the sake of progress is unnecessary, every returning spirit speaking of and affirming progress to be eternal in spirit life. The doctrine is contrary to any of the known laws of nature, which never returns upon its footsteps. All its circles are spirals – all its cycles upwards and onwards, never backwards or downwards. The oak never returns to be the acorn, the eagle never returns to be the egg.

Another quote from *The Unseen Universe:*

Question: Explain evolution of the soul, re-incarnation and re-embodiment?

Answer: My dearest friends, evidently the person who sent this question believes in re-incarnation – that the soul or spirit of man must return, enter the body, and live over again in order to evolve into higher condi-tions. Though I am a spirit, I do not recognize it in that way. I know nothing about a spirit coming a sec-ond time and taking itself a body and living again. If a spirit desires to learn more, and evolve more, it can do so without being re-incarnated in a human body.

The evolution of spirit is represented to you in many ways. The spirit of man today has evolved out of ignorance into light, and so will it be unto all eter-nity, for as I have said before, no spirit can stand still but must progress eternally. They must learn more and more of their own divine self. I say this because it has been understood that the divine is God and the spirit is of God, and must evolve higher and higher every day.

So friends, it is not necessary that spirits live another four score years and ten in a material body, but they can learn on the spirit side of life.

Although this was given by Emma Hardinge Britten over a century ago, it is as true today as it was then. Unfortu-nately however, times have changed in as much that the reincarnationists have spread their belief like a virus which has infected the West almost to the same degree as the East. The blind leading the blind!

Since the 1960's and the birth pangs of the so called 'New-Age' there has been an ever increase in the popularity of all and sundry attaching themselves to the movement, not least reincarnation and 'past lives'. In the UK and America, and elsewhere, sects and cults have been springing up like mushrooms attempting to please the wishes of the many, if not the masses, by such means as mixing Christianity with Spiritualism and adding Reincarnation and Past Life belief into the system. A less likely result than expecting to combine evenly oil, water and sand.

The usual problem with those attempting to try and ride two or more horses is that it results in a circus!

—⧜—

The Greater World Christian Spiritualist Association

The 'Greater World Christian Spiritualist League' (later to become 'The Greater World Christian Spiritualist Association') was founded on the 30th May 1931. It is an organisation of the Christ Mission to the four corners of the earth.

The inspiration for this movement, which resulted in Winifred Moyes dedicating her life to the work of the Greater World, came through her guide Zodiac, who was a teacher in the temple at the time of our Lord.

The Zodiac Messages (Reference Edition) was first published in 1965 by the GWCSA and consists of a volume of over 400 pages. It is based upon the messages of Zodiac. *The Zodiac Messages* have been translated into many languages and have been circulated throughout the world.

I quote from the DEDICATION in the book:

In gratitude to God who, in His great love, has sent this new light to us in our darkness; to those in Spirit, the servants of God, and especially His chosen servant and messenger Zodiac, through whom these messages were given; and in the sense of privilege that we have been called to give effect to the holy work of the Christ Mission, which is for all the world, we offer to Him – our Heavenly Father – in all humility and love, that which He has given, that He may bless, direct and use it to accomplish His Will, for the redemption and the raising up of mankind.

'The words that I speak unto you, they are Spirit, and they are life' (St.John 6,63).

The words in this book are 'life', for they point to man's rebirth into the kingdom of the Spirit.

And I quote from the PREFACE:

These Messages – so vast in their portrayal of Divine Truth, so revealing of the loving Purpose of God for all His Creation, would, if their spiritual significance were fully grasped, transform the world!

I will now quote from *The Zodiac Messages* exactly what Zodiac had to say on the relevant subjects of Reincarnation and Past Lives:

• Why the Theory of Re-incarnation Appeals to Many.

There are many in the world who are convinced that as the generations go on, the greater self within comes back to this earth in varied forms. You see, there has been much said which gives rise to this very natural explanation of the progress or the evolution of the soul. It appeals to commonsense! Man looks at himself and at his fellow beings, and his practical side acknowledges that neither he or they are ready for the powers of the Spirit, or for the joys of the Realms of Light. (*page 104*)

- **The Assumption that "Re-incarnation" only Provides a Workable Explanation of Man's Being; We Shall Not Enter Into a Physical Body Again.**

You will see dear children, that the physical mind has very good grounds for the assumption that 'Re-incarnation' only provides a workable explanation of man's being! Yet, as I have told you before, into a physical body you will not enter again; but the next body, in many cases, is not so dissimilar as you might think. Those who have neglected the opportunities provided on earth find their powers are very little greater; and those who have wilfully shut themselves off from the Light – which is all around – these are severely handicapped, and the physical body, when looked back upon, represents power and freedom indeed!

Once more I say: 'Get things in their right perspective', keeping always in mind the order, the magnificent order, of God's plans, the unparalleled justice of His laws and the infinite patience of the Father Himself, who waits and waits and waits! (*page 106*)

- **Present Misfortunes do not Indicate Errors in Past**

But in regard to your aura now and your present make-up, the mere fact that you may have a weak body, or perhaps not so able a mind as you desire, is no indication of failure in the past; and I would emphasize still more that the misfortunes which beset so many souls are not an indication of wrong-doing in previous lives in other worlds. That theory is one that has tortured many a humble striving soul, struggling along with a burden far too heavy for the physical make-up, but borne with patience by the strong Spirit within. (*page 205*)

—⁓—

CHAPTER 5

Albert G. E. Mobey

T.Eng. (CEI) AMIEE (retired)

For several years I corresponded regularly and frequently with Albert Mobey – or better known to me personally as Bert. He has been a valued friend and colleague of whom I have the greatest respect. A fine writer, correspondent and researcher into many aspects of the paranormal and we shared a great deal in the work. He, like myself was not afraid of speaking his mind and making clear to the world exactly where he stood. I still have boxes of our many letters together with audio and video tape recordings on such technical and instrumental subjects as EVP (Electronic Voice Phenomena) and experiments of infra-red photography for safe filming in a fully darkened seance room.

Bert is now well in his 80's and has suffered for a long time with Parkinson's disease and has had to go into a Nursing Home where he is being well looked after and is comfortable. I occasionally keep in touch with a phone call and he keeps in good spirit.

We were in agreement over the issue of reincarnation and he made no bones about it and what he considered to be so. Amongst the huge amount of paperwork, I have chosen the following extract from a letter which Albert Mobey sent as a personal letter to the Editor of *Psychic News* dated 21st. September 1989. It was personal and not for publication as he had included material concerning names of people still alive on earth. I have of course edited these out and include here only what he stated (word for word) on the subject of reincarnation.

Mr. Tony Ortzen (Editor)
Psychic News
20, Earlham Street
London
WC2 9LW

<u>Personal to Mr. Ortzen please.</u>

Dear Mr. Ortzen
.... The most significant issue about which there is conflicting information is:

Reincarnation is true/Reincarnation is not true.

This issue is the most significant because from a belief that reincarnation is true undoubtably flow endless imaginative possibilities that appeal very much to the ego, but do nothing to further Spiritualism because they cannot be proved. It is my opinion that survival can be proved to any reasonable person of good common sense. The contrary becomes self-evident when reincarnation is investigated. One immediately is in the position of having to accept authority that must not be questioned. Yet, at the same time, it is clearly implied that reincarnationist teachings come from higher sources and that those who presume to say '*The Emperor has no clothes*' are not spiritually developed to a high enough level. The ploy is as old as mankind.

Voices generated through the *direct voice* mediumship of Mr. John Campbell Sloan, when asked about reincarnation by Arthur Findlay replied that they had no knowledge of any such occurrence and had no teaching for it put to them from higher planes. Further, they could see no use that reincarnation could serve that was not better dealt with by use of the opportunities existing where they were. In short, the notion seemed absurdly futile and hardly worth giving serious thought to.

When Winifred Moyes' trance personality *Zodiac* was asked about reincarnation, his answer virtually was the same. He particularised that he had been where he was since his death from earth life, in which he was contemporaneous with Jesus, and no one he had contact with had reincarnated; neither did he know anyone who claimed that they had.

Dr. Carl A.Wickland, in his book *Thirty Years Among The Dead,* reports conversations with trance personalities who, when manifesting through his wife, go into close detail about the unholy mess discarnate spirits found themselves in as result of any detailed and firmly held belief in the notion of reincarnation, when alive in body or any erroneous earth-generated conviction, it would appear. If one accepts Dr. Wickland's report of the occurrence, even the High Priestess of reincarnation Mrs. H.P. Blavatsky took considerable trouble to spell out how wrong she had been to preach it and how much difficulty she was in as a result. 'Reincarnation is not true' she apparently said.

From the more esoteric source of OAHSPE we have not only detailed and categoric denials of the notion of reincarnaion, but a detailed account of how and why and by whom the belief was started. You might agree that if one is concerned about the moral fibre and physical condition of the amanuensis, as a guide for beginning to test any information from spirit, it would be very difficult a find a person more suited by preparation and life experience than Dr. John Ballou Newbrough. And if one accepts Dr. Newbrough's account of the happening, the method chosen to transfer OAHSPE seems to positively remove it from any creative involvement of his mind. I also think it significant that the Schole typewriter used must have been one of the first sold.

Thus, we have three of the finest amanuenses for spirit communication reporting that reincarnation is not true. One spelling out that it is what could be called an evil construction, i.e. one specifically directed against God's creative intent. Yet, from the sixties, at least, the Spiritist Movement has been saturated with reincarnationists. With these people one cannot be a progressed soul UNLESS a belief in reincarnation is part of your 'knowledge'. Yet, as over the past decade it has become increasingly clear, the notion just cannot be proven. On the contrary, people like Joe Keeton, after more than 8,000 hypnotic regressions of subjects cannot say that one of them has in his opinion proven reincarnation. But he does have proof that material collected from his subjects when regressed beyond the birth experience(?) can be false in that the statements contain either data that is out of time-context with the reported experience or that clearly has been derived from this life experience, no matter how momentary and inconsequential it might have been. During this decade, investigations of popular stories of Indian origin that previously have been accepted as probably proving reincarnation, have thrown up the more likely possibility that in a nation riddled with daft beliefs, the subjects and their relatives had hopes of material benefit from stories told from information easily to hand to involved relatives.

So, why do we have so many people choosing to accept what are, in my opinion, often dubious (to say the very least) sources of spiritist information that propose reincarnation, rather than those of untainted kind that deny it? It seems self evident that human vanity coupled with an inflated ego is one reason; this being coupled with a very realistic fear of (accepting that the person believes in survival) cutting the umbilical cord to Mother Earth for continued experience in what, apart for some very limited outline information, is unknown and certainly uncharted territory. There also must be a great deal of pressure from earth-located invisibles of the nature dealt with by Dr. Wickland, who would have vested interest in keeping the notion alive so that they can have comfort and a continued sense of personal importance in hanging on to and stimulating the beliefs of those incarnate in the ways that they saturated their own minds with while in their earth body. That is, apart for more long term devious justifications for promoting the belief, of the nature discussed in OAHSPE. It often works, as Joseph Smith *The Mormon Imposter* discovered in different context when he came across *A Story Ready-Made to Hand* that had been written when he was a child, by a person named Spaulding.

When one has a whole continent (India) that for thousands of years seems to have been obsessed by the idea of personal karma linked to reincarnation, it clearly can be seen how corrupting this belief can become and how

convenient it can be for the families at the top of the spiritual and material dung-heaps that result, to use it to
maintain their status, generation after generation. In the
end it produces a whole continent of people that simply
cannot adapt to true science and technology because the
ways of using individual minds have been genetically
conditioned by generations of nonsense thought. I
suggest that if the notion of personal karma extending
beyond the grave ever had any esoteric significance, it
was because we do have the FACT of genetic inheritance
and its effect on each new-born life to contend with and
use to our advantage by means of the application of
provably TRUE knowledge; if we can summon-up the
courage and the common sense to do so.

In my earlier years of looking into spiritual matters
and religions, I had a strong instinctive dislike of the
notion of karma as believed in by Hindus, for example. I
never could see that two wrongs stood any realistic
chance of making one new right, nor that a punishment
for some wrong that is unknown, stood any similar
chance. I have read over the decades from when I, personally, became spiritually 'aware', the convoluted and
ingenious theories that incorporated karma coupled with
reincarnation to explain the nature of the Cosmos and
the changing patterns of life within it.

The conclusions that I have reached is that the simple
fact of world human population growth over the past
few hundred years, terminates any rational discussion
about a concept requiring even two earth lives per soul.
The numbers of people alive in a mortal body at any one
time, are growing exponentially now, and it has been
calculated that already we have passed the point when at
a moment there are more people than there have ever

been born up to a life-time ago. Also, according to Mr. Bob Ralph, current lecturer in Biology at the University of Aberdeen, in 1941 the world population was about 2.3 billion. Since then it has more than doubled to around 5.1 billion, and at the present rate of increase of about 2 per cent per year, it will be around 8.2 billion by 2025. So, in what is now approximating to an expected life-time (84 years) we shall have more than three times the people, leaving no time at all for the departed to even say 'hello' to those who have gone on, before they are a new-born infant again. As a general principle, generally to be applied, the notion of reincarnation manifestly now can be seen to be absurd. A conclusion Mr. Findlay came to, albeit for a different reason. What we are reduced to, to keep the concept alive, is the postulate that Almighty God is causing souls to be brought from planets to other stars in creation, to keep the pot boiling, so to speak. That is assuming a great deal more than can be supported by a suburban housewife 'remembering' that she was a Cathar a few hundred years ago. Such happenings and the stigmata associated with them, in my opinion can be more probably associated with the kind of possession investigated by Dr. Wickland.

About karma, I am going to repeat myself because I happen to think that coupled to the notion of reincarnation, it makes the most diabolically evil combination so far dreamed up as result of mankind's inability to comprehend why he is.

What clearly is obvious is the effect genetic inheritance has in determining that great numbers of those born out of inappropriate couplings, will suffer some serious physical and or mental disability. The effect of this often can be compounded by manifestation of the negative characteristic, in the parents and surrounding family. If we continue to accept Hindu notions, any such unfortunates should be left to suffer their deserved fate and, presumably, be free to generate the continuance of their misfortune to give the opportunity for other souls to suffer similarly. To put it baldly, like that, is to clearly point up the absurdity of the original notion, when one considers that the whole object of earth life is said to be a preparation for an eternal life for the spirit, after the death of the body releases it. What better preparation for a more splendid life after death of the body, than a perfect body to start it in? So why preserve an inheritance of clearly imperfect bodies and minds, when we have the freedom and the knowledge to cease it? And why continue to revere as a kind of up-to-date religious teaching a notion only found in peoples who only can continue to live within primitive lifestyles that breed poverty and ignorance and unalleviated suffering and cannot even find the courage to dispose of their sacred cows?

CHAPTER 6

Whose Memory?

Derek Anton-Stephens

Dr. Anton-Stephens is a psychiatrist whose publications include contributions both to Christian and medical journals. He has most kindly given me permission to include in my book extracts, or in full, his article which was published in the June 1994 edition of the publication *The Christian Parapsychologist* whose editor Canon Michael Perry has also given me editorial rights to use.

I have decided to include the major part of Dr. Anton-Stephens's article to provide the reader with a full understanding:

'I was talking recently with a young man who assured me that he was the reincarnation of his mother's father, and that he had memories of many previous lives on this earth. It was my professional opinion that what he told me was, in sad fact, a manifestation of illness – *not* because of *what* he said but because of the disordered and irrational manner in which he thought and felt about what it was he was saying. This distinction between thought 'content' and thought 'process' is important, and needs to be borne in mind in any consideration of psychological aberration – to parody an old song, *it ain't wot yer thinks but the way that yer thinks it* that matters on many occasions when one is considering psychiatric diagnosis.

Nevertheless, a belief in reincarnation is held by many millions of men and women living today, and, in one form or another, it forms a major tenet of both Hindu and Buddhist religious belief – providing a tenable explanation of the manifold vicissitudes of life on this planet and a potential source of comfort in the face of them.

The scope of this essay is limited and is concerned with speculation about *the nature of the evidence* which one finds adduced in favour of reincarnation within the literature of spiritualism and psychical research. In particular, it is concerned with the dilemma which would seem to face those who believe not only in reincarnation but also in the possibility of 'mediumistic' communication between the 'living' and the 'dead'. Both beliefs may, indeed, be logically valid; there is nothing inherently impossible in either (although, strictly, logical validity should not be equated with truth or falsity), but if a belief in 'communication' *is* held, it would seem to the writer that the evidence for reincarnation becomes significantly weakened. How, one is tempted to ask, is it possible to distinguish the memories of a previous life, as retailed by the now reincarnated individual, from the memories of some discarnate entity able to communicate those memories to a living person, endowed with unrecognised mediumistic abilities who in genuine ignorance then attributes them to his or her own previous life? If one discounts the possibility of communication between the living and the dead, the evidence for reincarnation does indeed have cogency. If, however, one is willing to accept the possibility of 'communication', the evidence in favour of reincarnation must lose some of that cogency. And, if one accepts neither hypothetical possibility, if one regards all memory as a function solely of a physical brain, there will be questions to be answered which, to the writer's knowledge, have not yet been addressed. But let no one under-estimate that brain! To contemplate its workings is to be filled with some-thing not far short of awe.

As a practising psychiatrist I have myself used various techniques to facilitate the recall of lost memories of past traumatic happenings – and let there be no doubt, such techniques do work. On one occasion so successful were they that the lady concerned not only recalled a long 'forgotten' and vicious attack made on her head where, many years before, she had been injured. She saw, with horror, the blood dripping on to her hands – I myself only saw the 're-created' wound on her scalp (and a colleague of mine was able to photograph similar 'stig-mata' on the bodies of formerly tortured prisoners of war). On another occasion a gentleman, who had been enabled to recall events of long ago with great effect, required quite strenuous efforts to get him back, as it were, from the Paris of two decades earlier, into his pres-ent-day environment.

There can be no realistic doubt that these recalled memories were genuine (indeed, 're-experienced' would be a better term than 'recalled'). The lady with her scar *had* been attacked, the gentleman who found it difficult to return *had* been in Paris. In spite of being 'forgotten', the memories had been preserved intact, and they related directly and personally to those who described them. It is, indeed, a common experience that we ourselves can be transported back in time in response to seemingly trivial stimulation of our sensory organs (particularly by scents and smells) and that we then re-experience, often very vividly, long-forgotten scenes and events. There are, indeed, those who claim that nothing is ever forgotten once it has been registered on our brains – the difficulty in remembering being only a matter of recall and recognition. One does not forget – one simply fails to remember.

Now, whatever else may be involved, those who claim experience of a previous life on earth (or elsewhere, for that matter) must be dealing with *memory*. It may be a memory of great vividness, amounting to a re-experiencing, but it is still memory. The person who tells us of a previous life in, say, ancient Egypt is not, at the time of telling us, <u>in</u> ancient Egypt. They are in twentieth-century London or Edinburgh or wherever; and without that person's twentieth-century brain and nervous system we would know nothing about *any* of their incarnational experiences – past or present. But that brain and that nervous system did not exist before parental reproductive cells united to form an embryo (and if one is awestruck on contemplating that *brain*, one's reaction on contemplating what happens within that *embryo* defies description). It is not possible for the memory of a previous incarnation to reside within that which did not exist when the claimed incarnation occurred. Where, then, could it reside? Whose memory is it?

If, for the moment, we leave on one side the medico-psychological answer, there would seem to be two (and probably only two) other answers. Either the memory is somehow or other a part of the endowment of the indwelling spirit or soul of the twentieth-century human body which tells us about it, or the 'memory' belongs to, or comes from, some other spiritual source or entity which is not the indwelling one but which can somehow or other transfer its memory to the twentieth-century man, woman or child who tells us about it. Both these postulated explanations involve a radically dualistic philosophy – 'body' and 'spirit' being independent entities which come together during any particular incarnation. This is an entirely respectable line of thought with a time-honoured lineage, but it is an inescapable one for those who accept reincarnation as a fact. The act of human conception creates the physical body, but for the reincarnationist it cannot create the spirit – the resultant human being must be a duality *ab initio*. The almost inevitable corollary of this is that 'spirit' (whatever one thinks of that term as denoting) can and must exist without necessarily 'dwelling within' a physical body – thereby allowing the memory of previous existence to be attributed to that spirit rather than to the physical brain of its current human body.

In an attempt to mitigate this stark dualism there are those who postulate the existence of a non-individualised repository of incarnational memories and who talk of a 'Cosmic Consciousness', of 'Akashic Records', or of a 'Book of Life' within which 'personalised' memory as we would envisage it does not need to exist, but from which such memory can be 're-assembled' and then abstracted. On this hypothesis, descriptions of previous incarnations would be true memories of genuine events but would not be the private possession of any individual, living or dead, except the twentieth-century man or woman who is somehow able to tap into the repository. And, indeed, if all one's experiences during life *are* recorded in detailed totality in some cosmic memory-bank, there would be no need to postulate a continuing-to-exist 'spirit' in order to account for the claimed affirmed to be those of the discarnate souls who communicate through them, at which point an observation is called for. Let us admit that (as in any walk of life) there are charlatans, tricksters and self-deceivers amongst those who claim to be mediums – but also that there are those who are none of these things; let us admit that some of the relevant literature can be banal and far from convincing – but, again, that not all of it is. Some of it is clear, consistent and (if one accepts the concept of 'communication' at all) cogent. It would be a foolhardy person who dismissed *all* the findings of psychical research on the grounds that he *knew* all of it to be spurious.

Now, whatever may happen at the 'other end of the line', if I may put it like that, the act of mediumship would appear to be a physical phenomenon, for which various explanations are offered (ranging from the pathological through the ridiculous to the almost sublime). There are, indeed, those who contend that a 'medium' is no more than a person with greater facility than average in utilising an ability which, in lesser degree, is inherent in all; and one can accept this statistical assertion without needing to subscribe to any particular theory about how it operates or what it is that a medium mediates. If this contention is correct, if mediumistic potential is part of ordinary human make-up but only well developed in some, it is not difficult to envisage a situation in which a man or woman, having that ability but lacking awareness of its nature, might indeed attribute to their own previous lives the 'extraneous' information picked up from the memory of a discarnate entity with which they were unwittingly in touch. The memory would be accurate, but it would not be theirs.

In this connection one notes the frequent reference in spiritualist literature to the need for potential mediums to 'sit for development' – the inference being that, although the potential may be inherent, the expertise in handling it has to be acquired. A secondary inference might well be that those who had not acquired that expertise could either mishandle their abilities or not realise even that they possessed them. Under such circumstances it must be a possibility that an inexpert medium would construe information derived from a discarnate source as originating in his or her own mind (and one meets the frequent assertion that much human intuition and inspiration has just such an origin). It seems feasible, though, to take the inference one stage further and to argue that if the 'communicated' information were of a biographical nature which bore no similarity to the recipient's own life, it might be construed as a memory of a previous life of the recipient himself; and particularly would this be so if the human being concerned had no knowledge of, or belief in, the claim made by spiritualism.

In saying this, the writer hopes he has done justice to the case that a spiritualist might make in this context. Obviously, though, there are other, entirely mundane, answers to the question of whose memory it is on which evidence for reincarnation is based. It is possible, even probable, that *some* of the memories of claimed previous existences have their source in knowledge acquired from already available material (books, TV programmes, radio, conversations) which has genuinely been 'forgotten', or from a vivid imagination such as skilful novelists draw upon (although the use of 'inspired' to describe such skills might be thought of as taking us back into the preceding paragraph). The apparently well-attested instances of very young children who describe memories of past adult lives do not, however, fit easily into these explanations – and neither do instances in which accurate knowledge of a language unknown to the recipient is shown.

Nevertheless, as the cases cited at the beginning of this essay exemplify, the ability of the human brain to store detailed memory is awe-inspiring in its complexity and effectiveness. But the brain can store only such things as have been registered upon it. That it can then re-organise what has been registered into endlessly new combinations is obvious to all of us who can remember our last dream; but the resulting fantasy, however far-fetched, is composed of elements within the life-experience of the individual concerned. (To take a very simplistic example, I have never dreamt in whatever language it is that Tibetans or Eskimos use). If, then, someone – particularly a young, untutored child – describes memories of places and events which have no counterpart in its own experience, or in the experience of those from whom it might have acquired such knowledge at second hand, it is a reasonable assumption that one is not dealing with a brain-based memory. And especially would this be so if the memory includes a language foreign to the person doing the remembering.

One explanation which is not tenable, however, is that all reincarnational phenomena are the result of mental illness. It is of course the case that some psychotic patients claim to be historical personages. I myself have fond memories of Cleopatra (a middle-aged lady who cared in an exemplary fashion for ageing parents, the Pharaoh of Egypt and his Queen) and of the "Sharina of Persia" (whose embroidery attracted the attention of an expert in ancient Persian culture). I have also had the intriguing experience of two Jesus Christs who were able to tolerate, if not actually enjoy, each other's company. Without question, these good people were victims of illness (and on grounds other than their assumed identities). None of them could produce remotely accurate accounts of the lives led by those they claimed to be, and they were not bothered to explain how they came to find themselves where they were (although the lady who insisted she was Mary Queen of Scots did blame the then occupant of the throne for neutralising her claim to the Crown by having her declared insane).

And this state of affairs contrasts quite markedly with accounts given by those who have investigated claimants of reincarnation, and the detailed description they give of their previous lives. But even if this contrast were not so marked, the fact that some claimants can be shown to be mentally ill cannot be used to validate the inference that all of them are (perhaps the clearest impression one is left with after delving into the relevant literature is the tendency exhibited by some, on both sides of the debate, to draw universal conclusions from particular observations). It is also worth recording that in the writer's experience, no mentally ill person has claimed to be the reincarnation of a nonentity; the claimed identity has always been with a figure of historical interest or importance, And, in this connection, I may perhaps venture the personal comment that any claimed reincarnation of an important, famous or notorious figure should be treated with much suspicion. Quite apart from the sheer statistical improbability of such a happening, the element of 'grandiosity' in such a claim makes one think in purely psychological terms about the explanation of it.

I would, at this point, ask the reader to bear in mind the purpose of this essay. It is not a matter of arguing for or against reincarnation but of looking at the nature of the evidence on which judgments might be made. Some of the evidence cited in favour of it seems to be worthy of note, provided that one can accept the dualism involved and can overlook the fact that there is no explanation offered of *how* an independently existing 'spirit' comes to 'dwell within' a body and impress its memories on a brain. Some of the evidence strikes one as less convincing (for me, the results of hypnotic regression fall into this category – *not* because it doesn't work but because, paradoxically, it works almost too well) – and some of the evidence is frankly puzzling. Why is it, one wonders, that those who believe in, and practise, mediumistic communication with those who have died cannot, apparently, agree on the matter? Naively perhaps, one imagines that those with whom they are in communication might be expected to know the answer, one way or the other – but apparently this is not so. There is no unanimity of opinion on this matter in the reported communications received from those who assert that they have survived the death of their physical bodies.

One could offer speculative explanations for this rather curious situation. The Christian Church has the clear statement of its Founder that in his 'Father's House' there are 'many mansions', and it seems reasonable to suppose, as spiritualists insist, that the 'conditions' within those 'mansions' may not be identical, nor their inhabitants all of the same degree – thereby allowing for differences of experience and opinion. It is also insisted upon by spiritualist writers that the state of mind of many of those who have died is much the same (in respect of knowledge and belief) as it was while they were alive, and that enlightenment as to spiritual realities is not instantaneous, and may indeed be long delayed. It would seem to follow from this that some of those who communicate may, in what they say, be doing no more than repeating beliefs they held while alive – and the writer recalls a forceful attack made, in print, upon Hinduism and Buddhism on the grounds that both actually *condemned* their followers to reincarnation, because that was the firm belief they took with them. Nevertheless, and however one may view these hypothetical explanations, it does seem curious that there is no clear answer to be had from those who, in the nature of what they claim, ought to be in a position to give one.

There is one further, and final, point which is worth making. This essay has been concerned with reincarnation which, by definition, is a state of affairs which exists from the moment of birth (if not of conception itself). But the literatures both of psychology and of psychical research contain descriptions of individual human beings who would seem to have acquired apparently new identity and personality at some stage of their subsequent lives as adults. Dual and Multiple Personality is a recognised clinical phenomenon – and the writer has commented upon this intriguing situation in an earlier paper (*Demons and Daemons*). Its relevance, of course, is that here, too, one is sometimes presented with a set of memories which has no easily demonstrable connection with the life experience of the individual whose personality has become 'multiplied'. And, unless one regards any explanation other than a psychopathological one as untenable, here too the question arises – just whose memory *is* it to which one is listening?'

CHAPTER 7

A Famous Case Unveiled

—᙮᙮—

The Jenny Cockell Case
An Observation by James Webster

<u>SYNOPSIS:</u>

Jenny Cockell was born in 1953, married and has two (grown up) children, a son and daughter.

Mary (née Hand) married John Sutton, had eight children and lived in Malahide, Ireland. She died in Rotunda Hospital Dublin 24th. October 1932, a month after her daughter Elizabeth was born.

Jenny Cockell is fairly convinced that she is the reincarnation of Mary Sutton and claims to have met, and kept in touch, with several of these 'past-life' children (now in their well advanced years, having mostly been born during the 1920's, and some having already passed on).

—᙮᙮—

I will not expound the full story and evidence claimed in this case as there is plenty of reference matter to refer to and read. However, my intention is to bring to light a number of points on which to ponder, and to hesitate, before jumping into the deep end of the reincarnation theory.

So let us approach this like a detective and pose some pertinent questions:

- Why should a mother (Mary Sutton) logically desire to reincarnate on earth after 21 years in earthtime, to seek out her children, a further 39 years later (the age of Jenny Cockell when she began searching for them), only to discover that some had already passed over to the etheric world, and those remaining on earth would be in their 80's with time running out fast?

She would find herself stranded again and soon separated from her grown-up offspring. This time in a worse off situation because of becoming another person and personality – that of Jenny Cockell – who was to be married and have children of her own. Rationally, by remaining on the other side in the etheric plane, Mary Sutton would have already started to welcome her children over with what is generally accepted to be a wonderful reuniting of loved ones.

- And now for Jenny Cockell the question is what identity/personality does she maintain? Is she Jenny, Mary, or a combination, plus many other 'past-life' identities included? Mixed gender also? She mentioned being aware of other passed lives including one immediately before Mary, in Japan.

So when Jenny passes over this time to the etheric world, will she await to welcome her own children from this life as **their** mother? Surely yes. And what of Mary and her children reuniting from the previous life? Which mother are the Sutton offspring looking for? Is she expected to be Mary the mother of one generation and also Jenny the mother of the latest generation? But try and fit those two pieces of the jigsaw together! The mind boggles thinking of how many other personalities she is, to how many other souls?

This is only the start of the maze of confusion. Add thousands of permutations of relationships to this and one soon discovers what a mayhem a belief in the theory of reincarnation actually presents. It makes a mockery of survival of the individual conscious personality which once established, progresses through each stage of an onward journey with no retrace.

Summing up:

There are a number of inaccuracies, flaws and weaknesses in the Jenny Cockell case, some of which Jenny herself admits and can be referred to.

It could be that Jenny Cockell does not believe in 'life after death' and the continuance of the individualised personality surviving in other spirit planes. If this is so she could have been blocking, under hypnosis, with her own mind thinking (ref: page 11 'Between Lives' *Reincarnation International* January 1994). This is a matter of some important relevance I feel.

The far more obvious and likely probability is that Jenny – she has a very high IQ and is a member of MENSA – will have tuned in with her mind to Mary Sutton in spirit, even from her childhood, and was confusing the psychic and mediumistic communications from the entity with her own intellectual consciousness, and attempting to make it fit with her own boundaries of analytical thinking i.e. considering herself to be a reincarnation of someone else. This was amplified with the visits she made to the hypnotist, for regression, which itself is a questionable and unreliable methodology. This simply placed her own willingness into far clearer perspective.

—⸈⸈—

References:
Yesterdays Children by Jenny Cockell
        (Piatkus Publishers Ltd.)
Reincarnation International January 1994
The Time, The Place Anglia Television

CHAPTER 8

The Druze and Reincarnation Research in Lebanon

An Observation by James Webster

To The Ends Of The Earth— TV Channel 4
shown on 18th. May 1998
Featuring Roy Stemman: Editor of
Reincarnation International Magazine
Dr. Chris French: Psychologist from
Goldsmith College   London

—⁓—

Dr. Chris French stated; 'I would love to believe that death was not the end.' But he went on to make it quite clear during the programme that he was a complete sceptic of survivalism and the paranormal, as a whole, and not just with the issue of reincarnation and past-life evidence. So perhaps he was represented as a rather unsuitable partner with Roy Stemman for this research venture.

Roy Stemman stated that he believed in immortality and was in Lebanon to try and prove this through rein-carnation evidence.

Unfortunately such opposing argument, as I have discovered for myself as a researcher, can become sterile and provokes no real outcome as it tends to cancel itself out leaving a void. The third and more important factor involves other routes in attempting to 'prove' survival rather than with reincarnation and past-life evidence.

The Druze believe that the soul, immediately after physical death, is reborn into another body from the womb. That they have lived thousands of Earth lives before and reincarnate within their own religious culture, country or community. This was made obvious during the programme.

Half a million Druze from all walks of life are sure they will reincarnate. They have a history of persecution as a militant race. They are a religious sect in Syria and Lebanon sharing certain characteristics in common with the Muslims. Ismail al-Darazi, 11th. Century Muslim leader, founded the sect. Reincarnation is their firm belief. It is therefore quite obvious that the upbringing of children will be to encourage (indoctrinate) them into the belief system to accept without question.

All children are very impressionable everywhere in the world. Those brought up with strict religious conduct will be in a certain pattern of thinking. The Druze in Lebanon and the Hindus in India will have an automatic sense of acceptance and belief of reincarnation, karma, past lives and future lives on earth. The Druze do not even allow for an interim period between earth lives. And so one has to deduce that such people attached to this belief are in fact 'earthbound' quite literally. There is grave danger, with such dogged indoctrination, of trapping the unaware, without question, when taken to extreme.

In the television programme it was shown how children actually wanted, and were even encouraged by their parents, to be reunited with their alleged past-life families. This was obvious, particularly when it was believed that they were previously someone of importance. The question would then have to be proffered; How far back does one go? How many generations or past-lives? Is there really any belonging, relationship or family concept worth realising? Where is the fundamental love? It appears that a Pandora's box has been opened raising more questions than answers!

Such instances in the programme included the boy Rabih Abu Dyab who was considered to be the reincarnation of a famous football star and singer Saad Halawi, and Haneen Al-Arum a young girl believed to be the reincarnated wife of the old man Ajaj Eid.

It seems that there is often the tendency for reincarnationists to be more concerned with the past or the future rather than the ever present NOW.

The reincarnationist is deluded with trying to find a way forward in proving life-after-death through this by-way, and seems to be quite unaware or disinterested in the alternative routes which appear to me to be far more acceptable, convincing, positive, hopeful and spiritually inspiring and progressive. They seem to prefer the belief of further lives in a **physical** body rather than a state of freedom and spiritual progress being experienced through other planes of conscious existence with finer etheric and yet finer astral or spirit bodies.

A case of double identity:

Two boys were interviewed and both were claiming to be the reincarnation of Melhem Mlaheb who was killed by a shell whilst driving a bulldozer.

Chris French followed up the case of the boy who was said to have been frightened by a Pepsi Cola truck when two years of age. The boy claimed that he had worked for the Pepsi factory in his former life as a truck driver in which he was killed, and gave his name. However, when the supervisor of the factory truck drivers was called on the phone, he stated that he had worked at the factory for twenty years but had never heard of that employee by name.

Roy Stemman followed up the other case of a boy, also claiming to have been Melhem Mlaheb, who stated that his past life wife's name was Bassima and they had five children – Jihad, Ziad, Hanan, Jihan and Nahla.

They visited the memorial of the dead and found on a list the name and dates referring to Melhem Mlaheb and they tracked down the relatives of the man who confirmed that Melhem's wife was Amira **not** Bassima.

I cannot state whether or not the children fitted into any pattern of evidence, but the family of Melhem decided to accept the boy.

The above case and those relating to Haneen Al-Arum and Rabih Abu Dyab are documented in the TV programme and in published reports in Issue No: 15. June 1998 of *Reincarnation International*. I will not detail them further in this article but will present a few pertinent observations:

1. When Rabih Abu Dihab visited the football club to view memorabilia of the star player and singer Saad Halawi whom he was supposedly the reincarnation, he was very vague and required plenty of prompting which supplied obvious responses to mundane ques-

tions. The meeting arranged with the star player's close friend was unfortunately cancelled. Nothing of any specific or worthwhile evidential value came across.

2. If Rabih and his alleged past-life sister really were soul-mates as stated, there was nothing to show or testify this when they met. The young woman Samar was full of expectation and wishful thinking, whilst the boy looked somewhat vacant and ill at ease with the confrontation and negative until Samar supplied all the clues – 'Do you recognise me?' 'Don't I look like someone you know?' 'Are you upset with your past-life sister for not coming to see you?'

   The emotion came too late – the stable door was open and the horses had bolted!

3. The Haneen Al-Arum case is fully documented in *Reincarnation International Magazine* and shown on the film. My comment here would be for all the pro and anti explanations presented, the principle ingredient and possible if not probable explanation was so sadly missing. Neither Roy Stemman or Chris French seemed to be capable of providing the missing equation that in so many of these alleged cases of reincarnation, the children could simply be mediumistic and controlled or overshadowed by those in the spirit realms trying to get information across. Unfortunately the problem arises where there is a conflict between the religious upbringing of the child and belief system getting confused with spirit communication. Neither is clear and there is a breakdown in the result. The child is unaware of possible mediumship and encouraged by the parents and teachers to follow only the reincarnation and past-life formulae as

accepted in their religious belief. In effect, the brain computer is being fed information from two sources:

1. The mind (spirit communication).
2. Stored genetic memory, cultural and religious belief. The result is like two colours being mixed to produce an uncertain and unidentified third.

Roy Stemman, with enthusiasm, tries hard to convince Dr. Chris French whilst forever chasing rainbows and hoping the next case they researched would be the breakthrough and the pot of gold discovered, but which alas was not yet forthcoming. Rather like the football supporter with his team losing 3-0 but still chasing the ball with time running out! However, due credit should be given to Roy for admitting ; 'There is no such thing yet as a perfect case.' No doubt his zeal will keep him in the game with high hopes.

More observations:

It was interesting to note that the 'reincarnations' were always of the same gender as that of their alleged past-life, which is not in accord with most other reincarnationist beliefs.

It should be remembered that homosexuality is a crime and condemned in Islam. 'Gay' men and Lesbian women are not tolerated within their laws. It occurred to me that homosexuals could easily use the convenient let-out for their 'condition' if they claimed to have been a different gender in their past life. But it would seem that the Druze have taken careful consideration of that by keeping reincarnation and past and future lives within the framework of the law of their Moslem related religious tradition. So there is no change of gender and they return to remain within the 'comforts' of their own culture and community. One can also see where a kind of 'incestuous relationship' might occur and yet be quite acceptable.

With reference to another Channel 4 documentary 'The Miracle Police' screened on 28th. July 1998, part two of the programme was devoted to the 30% of Lebanese who are Catholic Christians and serve the Pope, Catholic Saints and Catholic approved Miracles. I noted that these were not mentioned in the documented reports in *Reincarnation International Magazine* or made any reference to during the TV documentary about the Druze. It occurred to me and made me wonder how many of this section of the population of Catholic Christians would state any belief or acceptance of reincarnation and past lives? How would children brought up in the 'faith' respond to such questions as put to the Druze?

Summing up:

I would say that the television programme about the Druze was a disappointment for reincarnationists and presented no real argument or substance to provide evidence in favour of reincarnation or past lives. Each case presented was hollow and questionable.

If the programme had included someone with a fine knowledge of spiritual philosophy, science and mediumship, a more likely explanation might well have been presented for every case. Chris French put *false memory* at the root of these cases which may have been correct, or at least in some cases, but no mention was made of other such probabilities e.g. cryptomnesia, partial possession, obsession and overshadowing, states of psychic or mediumistic experiencing, genetic memory, mind before brain (déjà vu) or what may well have simply been religious indoctrination and persuasion.

There was nothing, in my opinion, from the cases researched and shown in the documentary, to provide any credence in support of the reincarnation theory, which for all its increasing popularity, has presented itself, yet again, with a maze of confusion for all those who are enticed to enter into it.

CHAPTER 9

Researcher Arthur Oram

Arthur Oram was a fine researcher and respected member of the Society for Psychical Research who passed on in 2005 whilst I was in the process of researching and writing this book. I would like to thank Emma Blofield (daughter of Arthur Oram) who, on behalf of all Arthur's children, gave me permission to include extracts from their father's book *The System In Which We Live* and also for their kind good wishes for the success of my book.

I hold great respect for Arthur and his excellent endeavours, and have a copy of his book *The System In Which We Live* (published in 1998). I would like to quote extracts from the foreword written by Dr. Peter Fenwick:

Arthur Oram has had a lifelong interest in psychical research. For many years he was honorary secretary of the Society for Psychical Research and has a special interest in mediumship. His book is of significant interest as it looks at the deficiencies of our science from the point of view of a highly experienced and thoughtful parapsychological researcher who sets out to suggest a model that can integrate the scientific, objective world,

*subjective experience and parapsychological phenom-
ena, in a way that science at present is unable to do.*

*He argues for a multidimensional universe and
suggests that its higher dimensions manifest what we
experience as the qualities of mind. Arthur Oram's view
has many points in common with physicists such as
Bohm who suggest that there is an implicit order underlying the universe. Arthur Oram's model suggests that
mental and physical properties are all aspects of the same
physical world, but in different dimensions. This multidimensional concept is extremely powerful as it helps to
explain the relationship between parapsychological
phenomena, subjective experience, brain function and
the scientific, objective world.*

*As soon as our physical model of the universe is a
multidimensional system, life after death becomes a
possibility. Arthur Oram has much experience in inves-
tigating the claims of mediums, and points out the difficulties and vagaries of obtaining veridical information
through mediums. His experience and sensitivity makes
him ideally suited to take this look at the evidence for
personal survival after physical death.*

For the purposes of my book, I would like to quote some
extracts on what Artur Oram had to say, and comment
upon, regarding reincarnation. He devoted twelve pages
to the subject in Chapter 9 of his book *The System In
Which We Live.* I will now quote most of this chapter:

In order to consider reincarnation we have to be
prepared, at least for this purpose, to accept the idea of
survival, because otherwise reincarnation could not
come about, and we have to be prepared, again at least

for this purpose, to accept the idea of communication with the HD (*higher dimensional*) world, because otherwise we could not have obtained evidence for survival. Our model is well able to accommodate all of these requirements, but it can also support other factors which could make the acquisition of valid evidence for reincarnation more difficult than it might at first appear to be.

There is a substantial literature in the field of reincarnation. Professor Ian Stevenson has carried out extensive investigations and his reviews in Stevenson 1977 and 1982 provided convenient summaries of the situation regarding evidence before his masterly volumes Stevenson (1997a) and (1997b) became available. David Christie-Murray (1981) approached the subject from a wider base and included a bibliography of rather more than seven pages.

In the Myers scripts received by Geraldine Cummins it was stated (Cummins 1932, page 35) that:

> *Roughly, the newly dead may be divided into three categories:*
> *Spirit-man*
> *Soul-man*
> *Animal-man*

At page 40: Animal-man .... during his next incarnation he will probably either enter into the state of the soul-man, or he will at least be less of an animal ....and later, at page 63:

I shall not live again on earth.

It seems to be fairly clear that in general people do not remember earlier lives, but that cases where earlier lives appear to be remembered are more common in areas where there is a strong belief in reincarnation. It is just possible that, where an individual dies with a particularly strong conviction that he or she must reincarnate within a few weeks, months or years, the idea in itself produces reincarnation or something that appears for a while to be rather like it, whereas one who dies free from such conviction can proceed to develop in the HD world. There is an indication of this in the words of the New Testament at John 3,15:

Whosoever believeth in him should not perish but have eternal life

which suggests that the type of belief held by the individual is an important factor in breaking away from the cyclic development of 'animal-man' towards a progressive development that appears to be available for those who are ready for it. This statement might also be seen as disclosing some idea of the strength and potential of beliefs when held in this area, as has been demonstrated in much of Stevenson's work in recent years.

Some may object to the use of the term 'animal-man' on the grounds that animals frequently have higher standards of behaviour than the worst of humans. It looks, however, as if the distinction between animal-man and soul-man is not with regard to behaviour, but rather to the capacity for conceptual thought and viewed in this way there is almost certainly a valid and substantial difference in favour of the humans.

In those cultures in which there is a strong belief in reincarnation it is probably fair to say that it is generally held in connection with religious beliefs. In our own culture many people believe in reincarnation, but some of them do so as a result of facing situations that otherwise seem to them to be so unfair and so unjust and impossible otherwise to incorporate in any private model of an ordered existence. Such situations arise when a young child is injured for life, in many cases of disease and in other forms of hardship. It seems so difficult to understand how such situations can be allowed to arise, but with the concept of reincarnation and the availability of a number of separate lives it becomes easier to accept that such hardships might arise in one or two of them, to be balanced out by happier experiences in others. These arguments are important for those who hold them but they have no bearing on the question as to whether there is reincarnation or not.

Stevenson has found and recorded in his books instances of apparent evidence for reincarnation in which a child can draw upon memories for names, places and considerable further details relating to the life of an individual who has fairly recently died and whose family can be traced to confirm the evidence. However, in most of these cases, the child begins to lose these memories when about five or six years old and they have usually ceased before he or she reaches the age of eight (Stevenson, 1997b, page 6).

Stevenson used in titles of some earlier books the words 'Cases Suggestive of Reincarnation' and he has maintained this fairly open-minded approach. At page 11 of his summary volume of 1997 he writes:

A second paranormal explanation supposes that a discarnate personality controls or 'possesses' the subject .... This interpretation does not explain the almost invariable fading or amnesia of the child's apparent memories between the ages of 5 and 8 years .

This is only a part of Stevenson's discussion at this point, but it is a part that could be rather important.

It seems to me that a partial possession which can otherwise be referred to as a visiting mind is probably the correct answer. Again, it seems to me that reincarnation frequently takes place after a gap of very roughly 40 years, although it can take place quite quickly following the early death of a child or, apparently, of some individuals who have been mentally retarded, and then the new life can be that of a man or of a woman and normally carries no memories of the previous life. It appears that particularly where there is an overwhelming belief in an early reincarnation there can be this temporary partial possession of a new-born child, possibly initiated from the time of conception, and that from such time as the child needs to have full confidence in living and managing its own life (say around the ages 5 to 8) the visiting entity is withdrawn, to start living its own life in the HD world. I see this procedure as a whole, as a possible compromise organised from the HD world to overcome what would otherwise be the problem of dealing with the effect of a very strong belief in early reincarnation. I should however warn the reader that this paragraph and some of what follows on this subject comprises a mixture of speculation mingled with suggestion by others.

Even the term partial possession may be too strong. A visiting contact might be a better description. On the 5th. March 1998 I had a sitting with Marie Cherrie and for about half an hour I had a discussion purporting to be with a man who had been a professor of philosophy, on the question as to whether Stevenson's cases represent, in the main, reincarnations. I had met this communicator occasionally, but did not really know him and had no idea as to what bias, if any, his views might carry. He felt fairly strongly that not many of Stevenson's cases represent reincarnation. In the main he felt that they were based on communication.

A week later I had another sitting with the same medium and a whole hour of communication purporting to be with Dr. E.J. Dingwall whom I had known for many years and particularly in 1985, about a year before his death. I had communicated with him a number of times, but not often in recent years. He felt that reincarnation played little part in the Stevenson cases. He stressed that when a mother who believed deeply in reincarnation had a child with birth defects she would immediately be wondering who had reincarnated and would be making enquiries as to who it might have been. In this way he felt that some of the links would have been initiated in that way rather than by the child when he or she started to talk.

Several Minds with One Body?

We probably tend to overlook the extent to which we can reflect the work and thinking of many minds that come for a while to help us, without at any time divulging their identity or even their presence or existence. For my own part I had such help in becoming particularly skilled for one so young, at drawing complicated patterns with a compass on sheets of paper about the size of our present A3, and I lost that particular skill and knew at the time that I had lost it, some time before I was six. I record this here from memory and in the absence of records or relics of those times. It so happens that my memories of that ability and of what it felt like to lose it and to know that I had lost it have remained surprisingly clear for so many years. Such considerations have encouraged me to favour the hypothesis that Stevenson's cases have in the main been of the partial-possession type rather than reincarnations. My preliminary and so far inadequate delvings into his monumental work of 1997 seem to strengthen that approach.

It has been suggested elsewhere that a normal healthy individual can have a number of attendant minds working with or alongside his own mind. His own mind is the central one and is normally in control. It appears that the others can have any of a number of grades of status and lengths of stay. The 'guide', familiar to those who have sittings with mediums, is just one rather advanced grade and can be with an individual for many years. It was suggested by Swedenborg that some of a less advanced grade may not realise that they are associated with a living person, and even that there can occasionally be difficulties if they find out. We do not know about that, but some people know about the problems that arise in cases of multiple personality, where a secondary mind takes control from time to time, and about the problems of possession where a secondary mind takes control to a greater or less extent and makes the victim ill, or even mad. Wickland (1924) described the work he did in treating patients suffering from possession.

Demonstrations of the removal under hypnosis of obsessing minds that are causing illness and damage to an otherwise healthy individual can be impressive and there are many therapists offering such treatment. It seems, however, to be unfortunate that there is a growing tendency to include high-sounding assertions of the activities of so-called 'extraterrestrials'. If entities of that nature are causing trouble, then it will obviously be wise to try to remove them, but the powerfully worded assertions that they play an important part may cause a great deal of trouble through suggestion. To this extent such work could be creating some of the conditions it claims to treat. Partial obsession by what are referred to by some therapists as 'attachments' appears to be an important source of trouble for many people and its handling an important aspect of required treatment. The victims of violent death in war appear to be responsible for much of the trouble.

Therapists, however, normally make no attempt to verify the identities of the misplaced minds that have been causing the trouble. Their objective is to cure their patients of a wide variety of problems that can arise from interference by 'attachments'. It is extremely important that such therapy should not only get the unwanted attachment out of the body of the patient, but that it should be guided successfully to a proper and relatively permanent place in the HD world. Unless this is handled effectively the unwanted possessing mind will merely find another body it can become attached to. Wickland handled all of this through his wife who was a medium, but to-day most of those operating in this field handle all aspects of the work through the patient, under hypnosis. This obviously calls for advanced skills in hypnosis as well as in the handling of this particular type of therapy.

Hypnosis can apparently be used to regress the patient back to his or her earlier lives, but that is in effect a different subject. Some might regard that work as calling for careful attention to the identity of the earlier lives, but in practice it is probably almost impossible to obtain such evidence. If there is a mind helping from within the HD World, that mind has the choice of producing a genuine earlier life, or an imagined one, or some other earlier life, just to satisfy the enquirer and help him in that way. Checking with historical evidence might occasionally help to identify such a life, but probably will not do so, because any amount of detail can be recalled and we normally have no means of checking the means that has been used to produce it.

All of this has been handled here under a chapter heading that deals with reincarnation. It could have been placed elsewhere in this book, but it has subtle connections with the work of Ian Stevenson in that it is another way in which we can meet problems arising from the inability of those dying, usually through violence, to find their proper places in the HD worlds. It is not reincarnation but it does represent important ways in which an individual can be deflected towards, what may seem to him, in his seriously troubled state following a violent death, as being something like reincarnation. At least they are different ways of becoming associated with a body, however much trouble they may cause.

Our main conclusion must be that we do not know much about reincarnation, in spite of the enormous amount of highly professional work that has been done on the subject.

Many situations that look like reincarnation could possibly arise from the activity of visiting minds who are with us for a while and then move on.

It could be that for some of those who die with a strong conviction that they then have to reincarnate, the 'visiting mind' situation might be used for a while, as a weaning process, so that they can, after a relatively short period, be introduced to the full life of the HD world.

It looks as if the 'memories of earlier lives' obtained with the help of hypnosis or by other methods could be:

(i) Memories of earlier lives of that individual, or
(ii) Communications selected or designed to meet the experimenter's or the individual's requirements.

We probably have no way of distinguishing between these two possibilities, and checking details against historical records is almost certainly irrelevant for that purpose because the minds that are making the arrangements presumably have some freedom of choice as to what they produce.

CHAPTER 10

Philosophy, Religion
and Spiritual Teaching

Jiddu Krishnamurti (1895 - 1986)

For more than sixty years Krishnamurti travelled the world giving public talks and private interviews to thousands of people of all ages and backgrounds, stating that only through a complete change in the hearts and minds of individuals can there come about a change in society and peace in the world. He passed on, from this world, at the age of ninety and his talks, dialogues, journals and letters have been preserved in more than seventy books and in hundreds of audio and video recordings.

Because of the very serious nature of the issues Krishnamurti raised, he felt it was of primary importance that those interested in inquiring with him begin their investigation in the right spirit. He reminded his audience that he was not trying to convince them of anything, nor was he an instructor.

One of the best introductions to his work is the three volume set *Commentaries on Living*.

Krishnamurti had been groomed by Annie Besant to become the new world teacher with heavy involvement of the Theosophical Society. In 1926 he became the President of the Theosophical Educational Trust.

But then in the summer of 1929 at the opening talk of the Ommen Camp in Holland Krishnamurti announced publicly before a large audience, the dissolution of The Order of the Star and declared that 'truth is a pathless land', that henceforth he wanted no followers, and that his only concern was to set men free from the bondage of all religions, beliefs and fears, as he had set himself free. In 1930 he decided to resign from all organisations including the Theosophical Society.

My own personal interest in Krishnamurti came about during the 1970's when a friend in Tunbridge Wells introduced me to the profound philosophy of this teacher. I felt a need to get to grips and understand more. Later on and for several years until just prior to his passing (1986), my wife and I travelled to Brockwood Park in Hampshire for the annual gathering to listen to Krishnamurti speak in the great marquee. We would pitch our tent (and later a caravan) in the lovely grounds which surrounded the school and centre of the Krishnamurti Foundation Trust, with the many other campers who had arrived from all around the world. There was a wonderful feeling of tranquility and 'oneness' which seemed to transcend everyday living.

I remember once at a Brockwood gathering when Krishnamurti had been discussing how organised religion and belief systems become fragmented, he told the following rather touching little story which went rather like this:

It was a lovely sunny day and my friend was walking along the road with the devil, busy in discussion, when my friend noticed a man walking in front of them who suddenly stopped and bent to pick up something from the road. My friend said to the devil 'what has that man picked up?' And the devil replied 'He has picked up Truth.' 'Oh' said my friend 'that must be bad news for you?' 'Not at all' replied the devil 'I am going to help him to organise it.'

We have collected many books, tapes and videos over the years of this quite unique philosopher and without doubt, I would say, it has made my wife and myself far more observant, attentive and ready to question and enquire deeply into everything – not least ourselves.

Krishnamurti, in an address on the need of individual freedom of thought, declared that the theory of reincarnation is a theory of the lazy, and urged liberation from all dogma. (ref: p.218 *The Gateway of Understanding* by *Dr. Carl Wickland*)

The following is from *Questions and Answers* by J. Krishnamurti published in January 1982 by *The Krishnamurti Foundation Trust Ltd.*

Chapter 17 REINCARNATION

Questioner: Would you please make a definite statement about the non-existence of reincarnation since increasing 'scientific evidence' is now being accumulated to prove reincarnation is a fact. I am concerned because I see large numbers of people beginning to use this evidence to further strengthen a belief they already have, which enables them to escape problems of living and dying. Is it not your responsibility to be clear, direct and unequivocable on this matter instead of hedging round the issue?

Krishnamurti: We will be very definite. The idea of reincarnation existed long before Christianity. It is prevalent almost throughout India and probably in the whole Asiatic world. Firstly: what is it that incarnates; not only incarnates now, but reincarnates again and again? Secondly: the idea of there being scientific evidence that reincarnation is true, is causing people to escape their problems and that causes the questioner concern. Is he really concerned that people are escaping? They escape through football or going to church. Put aside all this concern about what other people do. We are concerned with the fact, with the truth of reincarnation, and you want a definite answer from the speaker.

What is it that incarnates, is reborn? What is it that is living at this moment, sitting here? What is it that is taking place now to that which is in incarnation?

And when one goes from here, what is it that is actually taking place in our daily life, which is the living movement of incarnation – one's struggles, one's appetites, greeds, envies, attachments – all that? Is it that which is going to reincarnate in the next life?

Now those who believe in reincarnation, believe they will be reborn with all that they have now – modified perhaps – life after life. Belief is never alive. But suppose that belief is tremendously alive, then what you are now matters much more than what you will be in a future life.

In the Asiatic world there is the word 'karma' which means action in life now, in this period, with all its misery, confusion, anger, jealousy, hatred, violence, which may be modified, but will go on to the next life.

So there is evidence of remembrance of things past, of a past life. That remembrance is the accumulated 'me', the ego, the personality. That bundle, modified, chastened, polished a little bit, goes on to the next life.

So it is not a question of whether there is reincarnation (I am very definite on this matter, please) but that there is incarnation now; what is far more important than reincarnation, is the ending of this mess, this conflict, now. Then something totally different goes on.

Being unhappy, miserable, sorrow-ridden, one says: 'I hope the next life will be better.' That hope for the next life is the postponement of facing the facts now. The speaker has talked a great deal to those who believe in and have lectured and written about reincarnation, endlessly. It is part of their game. I say, 'All right, Sirs, you believe in it all. If you believe, what you do now matters'. But they are not interested in what they do now, they are interested in the future. They do not say: 'I believe and I will alter life so completely that there is no future'. Do not at the end of this say that I am evading this particular question; it is you who are evading it. I have said that the present life is all-important; if you have understood and gone into it, with all the turmoil of it, the complexity of it – end it, do not carry on with it. Then you enter into a totally different world. I think that is clear, is it not? I am not hedging. You may ask me: 'Do you believe in reincarnation?' Right? I do not believe in anything. This is not an evasion. I have no belief and it does not mean that I am an atheist, or that I am ungodly. Go into it, see what it means. It means that the mind is free from all the entanglement of belief.

In the literature of ancient India there is a story about death and incarnation. For a Brahmin it is one of the ancient customs and laws, that after collecting worldly worth he must at the end of five years give up everything and begin again. A certain Brahmin had a son and the son says to him, 'You are giving all this away to various people, to whom are you going to give me away; to whom are you sending me?' The father said, 'Go away, I am not interested.' But the boy comes back several times and the father gets angry and says; 'I am going to send you to *Death*' – and being a Brahmin he must keep his word. So he sends him to *Death*. On his way to *Death* the boy goes to various teachers and finds that some say there is reincarnation, others say there is not. He goes on searching and eventually he comes to the house of *Death*.

When he arrives, *Death* is absent. (A marvellous implication, if you go into it.) *Death* is absent. The boy waits for three days. On the fourth day, *Death* appears and apologises because the boy was a Brahmin; he says, 'I am sorry to have kept you waiting and in my regret I will offer you three wishes. You can be the greatest king, have the greatest wealth, or you can be immortal.' The boy says, 'I have been to many teachers and they all say different things. What do you say about death and what happens afterwards?' *Death* says, 'I wish I had pupils like you ; not concerned about anything except that.' So he begins to tell him about truth, about the state of life in which there is no time.

—❦—

The Bahá'í Faith

The Bahá'í Faith is an independent world religion formed during the mid nineteenth century in Persia. With more than five million adherents residing in over 124,000 localities, the Bahá'í Faith is established in 204 countries across the world. The spiritual principles of the Bahá'í Faith affirm its overall purpose – to bring about the oneness of humanity. In co-operation with these same principles, Bahá'ís also believe that there is only one Creator and that the spiritual truth of all religions is the same.

The Bahá'í Reference Library

The Bahá'í Reference Library is an agency of the Bahá'í International Community, a non-governmental organization that represents and encompasses the world-wide membership of the Bahá'í Faith.

Extract from *Some Answered Questions*
Author: Abdu'l-Bahá
Source: U.S. Bahá'í Publishing Trust 1990

81: REINCARNATION

Question: What is the truth of the question of reincarnation, which is believed by some people?

Answer: The object of what we are about to say is to explain the reality – not to deride the beliefs of other people; it is only to explain the facts; that is all. We do not oppose anyone's ideas, nor do we approve of criticism.

Know, then, that those who believe in reincarnation are of two classes: one class does not believe in the spiritual punishments and rewards of the other world, and they suppose that man by reincarnation and return to this world gains rewards and recompenses; they consider heaven and hell to be restricted to this world and do not speak of the existence of the other world.

Among these there are two further divisions. One division thinks that man sometimes returns to this world in the form of an animal in order to undergo severe punishment and that, after enduring this painful torment, he will be released from the animal world and will come again into the human world; this is called transmigration. The other division thinks that from the human world one again returns to the human world, and that by this return rewards and punishments for a former life are obtained; this is called reincarnation. Neither of these classes speak of any other world besides this one.

The second sort of believers in reincarnation affirm the existence of the other world, and they consider reincarnation the means of becoming perfect – that is, they think that man, by going from and coming again to this world, will gradually acquire perfections, until he reaches the inmost perfection. In other words, that men are composed of matter and force; matter in the beginning – that is to say, in the first cycle – is imperfect, but on coming repeatedly to this world it progresses and acquires refinement and delicacy, until it becomes like a polished mirror; and force, which is no other than spirit, is realized in it with all the perfections.

This is the presentation of the subject by those who believe in reincarnation and transmigration. We have condensed it; if we entered into the details, it would take much time. This summary is sufficient. No logical arguments and proofs of this question are brought forward; they are only suppositions and inferences from conjectures, and not conclusive arguments. Proofs must be asked for from the believers in reincarnation, and not conjectures, suppositions and imaginations.

But you have asked for arguments of the impossibility of reincarnation. This is what we must now explain. The first argument for its impossibility is that the outward is the expression of the inward; the earth is the mirror of the Kingdom; the material world corresponds to the spiritual world. Now observe that in the sensible world appearances are not repeated, for no being in any respect is identical with, nor the same as, another being, The sign of singleness is visible and apparent in all things. If all the granaries of the world were full of grain, you would not find two grains absolutely alike, the same and identical without any distinction. It is certain that there will be differences and distinctions between them. As the proof of uniqueness exists in all things, and the Oneness and Unity of God is apparent in the reality of all things, the repetition of the same appearance is absolutely impossible. Therefore, reincarnation, which is the repeated appearance of the same spirit with its former essence and condition in this same world of appearance, is impossible and unrealizable. As the repetition of the same appearance is impossible and interdicted for each of the material beings, so for spiritual beings also, a return to the same condition, whether in the arc of descent or in the arc of ascent, is interdicted and impossible, for the material corresponds to the spiritual.

Nevertheless, the return of material beings with regard to species is evident; so the trees which during former years brought forth leaves, blossoms and fruits in the coming years will bring forth exactly the same leaves, blossoms and fruits. This is called the repetition of species. If anyone makes an objection saying that the leaf, the blossom and the fruit have been decomposed, and have descended from the vegetable world to the mineral

world, and again have come back from the mineral world
to the vegetable world, and, therefore, there has been a
repetition – the answer is that the blossom, the leaf and
the fruit of last year were decomposed, and these
combined elements were disintegrated and were
dispersed in space, and that the particles of the leaf and
fruit of last year, after decomposition, have not again
become combined, and have not returned. On the
contrary, by the composition of new elements, the species
has returned. It is the same with the human body, which
after decomposition becomes disintegrated, and the
elements which composed it are dispersed. If, in like
manner, this body should again return from the mineral
or vegetable world, it would not have exactly the same
composition of elements as the former man. Those
elements have been decomposed and dispersed; they are
dissipated in this vast space. Afterward, other particles of
elements have been combined, and a second body has
been formed; it may be that one of the particles of the
former individual has entered into the composition of the
succeeding individual, but these particles have not been
conserved and kept, exactly and completely, without
addition or diminution, so that they may be combined
again, and from that composition and mingling another
individual may come into existence. So it cannot be
proved that this body with all its particles has returned;
that the former man has become the latter; and that,
consequently, there has been repetition; that the spirit
also, like the body, has returned; and that after death its
essence has come back to this world.

If we say that this reincarnation is for acquiring
perfections so that matter may become refined and deli-
cate, and that the light of the spirit may be manifest in it

with the greatest perfection, this also is mere imagination. For, even supposing we believe in this argument, still change of nature is impossible through renewal and return. The essence of perfection, by returning, does not become the reality of perfection; complete darkness, by returning, does not become the source of light; the essence of weakness is not transformed into power and might by returning and an earthly nature does not become a heavenly reality. The tree of Zaqqum *(the infernal tree mentioned in the Qur'án)*, no matter how frequently it may come back, will not bring forth sweet fruit, and the good tree, no matter how often it may return, will not bear a bitter fruit. Therefore, it is evident that returning and coming back to the material world does not become the cause of perfection. This theory has no proofs nor evidences; it is simply an idea. No, in reality the cause of acquiring perfections is the bounty of God.

The Theosophists believe that man on the arc of ascent *(i.e. of the Circle of Existence)* will return many times until he reaches the Supreme Centre; in that condition matter becomes a clear mirror, the light of the spirit will shine upon it with its full power, and essential perfection will be acquired. Now, this is an established and deep theological proposition, that the material worlds are terminated at the end of the arc of descent, and at the beginning of the arc of ascent, which is opposite to the Supreme Centre. Also, from the beginning to the end of the arc of ascent, there are numerous spiritual degrees. The arc of descent is called beginning *(Lit., bringing forth)*, and that of ascent is called progress *(Lit., producing something new)*. The arc of descent ends in materialities, and the arc of ascent ends in spiritualities.

The point of the compass in describing a circle makes no retrograde motion, for this would be contrary to the natural movement and the divine order; otherwise, the symmetry of the circle would be spoiled.

Moreover, this material world has not such value or such excellence that man, after having escaped from this cage, will desire a second time to fall into this snare. No, through the Eternal Bounty the worth and true ability of man becomes apparent and visible by traversing the degrees of existence, and not by returning. When the shell is once opened, it will be apparent and evident whether it contains a pearl or worthless matter. When once the plant has grown it will bring forth either thorns or flowers; there is no need for it to grow up again. Besides, advancing and moving in the worlds in a direct order according to the natural law is the cause of existence, and a movement contrary to the system and law of nature is the cause of nonexistence. The return of the soul after death is contrary to the natural movement, and opposed to the divine system.

Therefore, by returning, it is absolutely impossible to obtain existence; it is as if man, after being freed from the womb, should return to it a second time. Consider what a puerile imagination this is which is implied by the belief in reincarnation and transmigration. Believers in it consider the body as a vessel in which the spirit is contained, as water is contained in a cup; this water has been taken from one cup and poured into another. This is child's play. They do not realize that the spirit is an incorporeal being, and does not enter and come forth, but is only connected with the body as the sun is with the mirror. If it were thus, and the spirit by returning to this material world could pass through the degrees and attain to essential perfection, it would be better if God prolonged the life of the spirit in the material world until it had acquired perfections and graces; it then would not be necessary for it to taste of the cup of death, or to acquire a second life.

The idea that existence is restricted to this perishable world, and the denial of the existence of divine worlds, originally proceeded from the imaginations of certain believers in reincarnation; but the divine worlds are infinite. If the divine worlds culminated in this material world, creation would be futile; nay, existence would be pure child's play. The result of these endless beings, which is the noble existence of man, would come and go for a few days in this perishable dwelling, and after receiving punishments and rewards, at last all would become perfect. The divine creation and the infinite existing beings would be perfected and completed, and then the Divinity of the Lord, and the names and qualities of God, on behalf of these spiritual beings, would, as regards their effect, result in laziness and inaction!

Such were the limited minds of the former philosophers, like Ptolemy and the others who believed and imagined that the world, life and existence were restricted to this terrestrial globe, and that this boundless space was confined within the nine spheres of heaven, and that all were empty and void. Consider how greatly their thoughts were limited and how weak their minds. Those who believe in reincarnation think that the spiritual worlds are restricted to the worlds of human imagination. Moreover, some of them, like the Druzes and the Nusayris, think that existence is restricted to this physical world. What an ignorant supposition! For in this universe of God, which appears in the most complete perfection, beauty and grandeur, the luminous stars of the material universe are innumerable! Then we must reflect how limitless and infinite are the spiritual worlds, which are the essential foundation.

But let us return to our subject. In the Divine Scriptures and Holy Books 'return' is spoken of, but the ignorant have not understood the meaning, and those who believed in reincarnation have made conjectures on the subject. For what the divine Prophets meant by 'return' is not the return of the essence, but that of the qualities; it is not the return of the Manifestation, but that of the perfections. In the Gospel it says that John, the son of Zacharias, is Elias. These words do not mean the return of the rational soul and personality of Elias in the body of John, but rather that the perfections and qualities of Elias were manifested and appeared in John.

A lamp shone in this room last night, and when tonight another lamp shines, we say the light of last night is again shining. Water flows from a fountain; then it ceases; and when it begins to flow a second time, we say this water is the same water flowing again; or we say this light is identical with the former light. It is the same with the spring of last year, when blossoms, flowers and sweet-scented herbs bloomed, and delicious fruits have come back, and those blossoms, flowers and blooms have returned and come again. This does not mean that exactly the same particles composing the flowers of last year have, after decomposition, been again combined and have then come back and returned. On the contrary, the meaning is that the delicacy, freshness, delicious perfume and wonderful colour of the flowers of last year are visible and apparent in exactly the same manner in the flowers of this year. Briefly, this expression refers only to the resemblance and likeness which exist between the former and latter flowers.

—⁓—

BUDDHISTS AGAINST REINCARNATION

This is a website I recently came across and considered it well worth including as it does indeed portray a rather surprising and yet profound attitude. The article reads as follows:

The Buddha clearly asked his followers not to believe things simply because he said them or they are stated in religious texts, but because you have experience of them being true. It follows therefore that there should be no pressure on the Buddhist to believe in reincarnation – from others or within themselves. Reincarnation is not one of the 4 Noble Truths and does not feature in the 8 Fold Path or Meditation.

This site is dedicated to encourage open free debate and thought on the issue of reincarnation (a term here used to mean 'Rebirth' at the point of death). We would like to make the following points derived from human experience:

1. **Hear no evil, see no evil, speak no evil**

It is true that some might gain significant reassurance from a belief in reincarnation and we should be sympathetic with this. People who need a belief will tend to defend it by ceasing to listen, switching attention, or being distracted by irritation and contempt. Hopefully they will not be harmed by this site. Perhaps they would choose not to read further.

2. Seeing is believing

To hold untrue beliefs has unpleasant side effects. Irrational beliefs are often in conflict with rational ones and this causes tension and suffering to the believer (Festinger Cognitive Dissonance Theory in psychology) – 'We learn things with great certainty through directly experiencing them via the senses.' – This human belief is in conflict with a belief in reincarnation (which few believers would claim to have any direct experience or evidence of). As there is no physical evidence for reincarnation there is little reason to believe in it.

3. Throwing the baby out with the bathwater

Human beings have a tendency to reject a group of associated ideas (as in the case of Buddhism) if they find just one of these ideas to be untrue. This means that intelligent people might reject Buddhism on the basis of their strong reasonable disbelief in reincarnation. This would be unfortunate.

4. 'It's not a religion'

Buddhism is not a religion yet it strays away from human observation into 'spiritual' territories when it deals with reincarnation and the human soul. It therefore puts itself in conflict with other religions which may disagree with that, for example, a human might come back as a goat after death. As a result many religious people may not, contemplate Buddhist beliefs simply because of its association with reincarnation. This is unfortunate as they may benefit from Buddhist ideas and practices.

5. 'Grasping'

A belief in rebirth can encourage thoughts and desires of surviving death. This grasping tendency leads to suffering (see 4 Noble Truths below).

6. Buddhism is subtle

The rebirth can be seen as metaphorical. Every day and every moment we change and are 'reborn' as the contents of our bodies, thought, memories and feelings change. In fact after 7 years there is very little original material left in a human. Most has been replaced. Buddhism is subtle but its simplified expression can be misleading.

7. The Messenger and the Message

The message of Buddha was carried orally for 100 years before being written down. It is unlikely to have remained unaltered in that time due to the limitations of human nature, intellect and memory. It should also be remembered that Buddha was a human being and was therefore able to be wrong as well as right about intellectual matters including Rebirth of consciousness at the point of death.

Buddha appears to reject the concept of Reincarnation

'There is rebirth of character,
but no transmigration of self,
Thy thought-forms reappear,
But there is no egoentity transferred.
The stanza uttered by a teacher
is reborn in the scholar who repeats the words.' (9)

'Thy self to which though cleavest is a constant change.
Years ago thou wast a small babe;
Then, thou wast a boy;
Then a youth, and now, thou art a man.
Is there an identity of the babe and the man?
There is an identity in a certain sense only.
Indeed there is more identity between the flames
of the first watch and the third watch,
even though the lamp might have been extinguished
during the second watch.' (57)

Reproduced from Chapter 53 *Gospel of Buddha*, a compilation of ancient texts published 1894 by Paul Carus.
Available on: www.mountainman.com.au/buddha/

The 4 Noble Truths

It seems that any discussion of Buddhism is incomplete without mention of the 4 Noble Truths, essence and origin of Buddhist thought. They are as follows:

1. **The Truth of Dukkha**
   All forms of existence are subject to Dukkha (stress, unsatisfactoriness, disease)

2. **The Truth of the Cause of Dukkha**
   Dukkha is caused by Tanha (grasping). The main cause of suffering is desire or craving. The failure to satisfy one's desire causes disappointment and suffering.

3. **The Truth of Cessation of Dukkha**
   Eliminate the cause of Dukkha (grasping) and suffering will cease.

4. **The Truth of the Path**
   The 8 Fold Path is the way to eliminate grasping/extinguish dukkha.

The 8 Fold Path

1. Right understanding
2. Right thought
3. Right speech
4. Right bodily contact
5. Right livelihood
6. Right effort
7. Right attentiveness
8. Right concentration

Buddha has the Last Say

'But if there is no other world and there is no fruit and ripening of actions well done or ill, then here and now in this life I shall be free from hostility, affliction and anxiety, and I shall live happily.'

The Buddha

Taken from *The Kalama Sutra* (published by Rowen and Littlefield)
   Also quoted on page 34 of *Buddhism Without Beliefs* by Stephen Bachelor.

CHAPTER 11

Present Day Scientist
Stephen Blake M.Sc.(Lond.)

I felt it a privilege to become acquainted with Stephen Blake in September 2003. I had really found someone not only of an intellectual and intelligent level to work with, but with a real understanding of what was required to counter the reincarnationists lording it over the whole Spiritualist Movement as well as the populous of the world in general.

Stephen, or more popularly known as Steve, holds a Master of Science degree and lives in Kent, England. I first spotted his excellent letter published in *Psychic World* (Sept.'03) to which I replied to him personally. He thanked me warmly for my remarks and generously gave me permission to use his letter in any way I thought fit. He also stated the following in his response to me:

'My original purpose was to draw attention to some underlying inconsistencies in the theory of reincarnation, but ended up with a more general refutation. I am still amazed that the doctrine of re-embodiment can be disposed of so easily. It illustrates the power of reason in psychic or spiritual matters and the need to examine the grounds on which people hold their beliefs.'

The following is the actual letter which Steve had published in *Psychic World* (Sept.'03):

'Permit me, once again, to make a few comments on the vexed issue of reincarnation.

We are advised by our spirit friends and teachers that our earthly experiences of time and space have no reality on the spiritual planes. A hundred years of our time is *as nothing* to them and that our earthly lives pass by within *the twinkling of an eye.* All unfolds within a *spacious present* and distinctions between time and space are without meaning. More prosaically what appears, to us, as a temporal sequence is simultaneous to them. When this fundamental truth is applied to the doctrine of reincarnation we find that the notion of continual re-embodiment of the human soul is a misconception.

From the principle of one manifesting in diversity we need only accept that the soul (or self) manifests on earth as the family of human souls whose purpose is the realisation of divine potential. To the soul this manifestation of human life is simultaneous and all incarnated lives are coexistent. To the incarnated soul, however, these lives are separated in time and space. Some exist now (contemporaneous lives), some have existed in the past (previous lives), and some will exist in the future (future lives). This is a phenomenon of the physical world.

At the human level physical events can be placed in temporal order by attaching a *date* but cannot be placed in spatial order except in the special case of a one-dimensional space. The incarnated soul, whose earthly vision is limited to three-dimensions, and experiences time as duration is inclined, therefore, to *order* human experiences in a purely temporal manner. This enables a person to claim that he or she has lived before, in a *previous body*, and may live again in a *future body;* a view which is sustained by our inability to establish normal communications across time. Since, in the case of *contemporaneous bodies*, nobody would claim to inhabit more than one body at the same time, a spatial equivalent of reincarnation has never arisen. Thus the doctrine of reincarnation implies that we can occupy different bodies at different times but not different bodies in different places. This result is without spiritual foundation because there is no reality to earthly concepts of time and space on the spiritual planes. Distinctions, there, between time and space are meaningless. The only sensible result would be that the human soul cannot occupy different bodies at different times, or different bodies in different places. The one implies the other.

We see, therefore, that the notion of continual re-embodiment of the human soul is a philosophical confusion based upon our limited temporal vision. Human souls who have lived in the past, and human souls who will live in the future are all different and unique members of the human family. Brotherhood and sisterhood is a universal reality.

When our earthly lives are completed we shall continue to progress (or regress) to more rarefied (or grosser) planes of existence, with those we love, as part of the spiritual unfoldment of humanity within a *spacious present*. When the *awakening* or *at-one-ment* occurs on the plane of the soul, all will re-unite simultaneously. There will be no missing souls. All lives would have passed within *the twinkling of an eye* and earthly notions of time, space and separation will be seen as illusions of the material worlds.'

In a further letter to me dated 23rd. October 2003, Steve made the following remarks:

'Some time ago I assumed that if reincarnation *did* occur it would be the exception rather than the rule. This position, I have come to realise, is illogical. Either reincarnation is a reality for everyone or it is a reality for no one. There is no middle ground.

Recently a spiritual paradigm, based on the relationship between the temporal and the eternal, and linking the physical with the spiritual, began to unfold in my mind. This paradigm shows that the notion of successive physical re-embodiment of the human soul is a completely meaningless and self-contradictory concept without physical, spiritual or religious foundation. I have said as much in my letters to *Psychic World* but in a less forthright manner. I do not wish to offend nor do I wish to swamp the reader with a mass of ideas. My plan is to proceed carefully and in stages. However, some provocation is in order. It is absolutely necessary that reincarnationists attempt to 'shoot down' my ideas. Only then can I expose their beliefs as misguided. Their best strategy would be to remain silent.

I am convinced that most reincarnationists in the spiritualist movement, though well-intentioned, are deeply confused. Their confusion arises from:

(a) A failure to recognise or understand the relationship between the temporal and the eternal.

(b) Profound confusions about the nature of the human soul.

(c) A misuse of, or misunderstanding of language.

Re-read the first parts of M.G's letter to *Psychic World* (October). You will notice that she shies away from any discussion of 'time' beyond the physical, misuses the word 'focus' both in meaning and in application and has rather vague ideas about the nature of her spirit contacts. This may or may not be typical. We shall have to wait and see.

My ultimate purpose is to demonstrate that reincarnationism and materialism are manifestations of the same doctrine – that the human soul is mortal and that we all face death and oblivion. The only difference between the two dogmas is the number of incarnations involved before the soul perishes. In materialism the soul (if there is one) perishes at the end of the first physical life. In reincarnationism the soul perishes at the end of a succession of lives – but perish it does! If our reincarnationist friends knew what they were subscribing to they would drop the idea pretty quickly. I intend to enlighten them.

My letter to *Psychic World* (November issue) does not deal, specifically, with the aforementioned point. It is mostly in reply to the letters from Ms. A.G. and Mr. T.S. Following a further clarification of the spiritual paradigm, introduced in the previous letter, I continue to develop the arguments against reincarnation in a mathematical and scientific vein. Although the style is informal the logic is watertight. I have attached a copy of the letter to give you a preview.

Naturally there is a limit to how far the arguments can be taken within the confines of the letters page – but I have done my best.

Best wishes
Steve

The following is Stephen Blake's copy of his letter sent to *Psychic World* and published in the November '03 issue:

To: The Editor
Psychic World
8th. October 2003

Dear Mr. Taylor

Please allow me to respond to the thought provoking comments by *A.G.* and *T.S.* (October) to whom I offer my thanks.

To clarify the spiritual paradigm outlined in my previous letter (September) we observe that there is only one reality: Unity with God in the 'spacious present'. At the separation, the soul (or self) becomes the universe of souls and manifests as the cosmos. The cosmos or 'body of manifestation' is established as an 'idea construction' in the 'spacious present' and the created forms endowed with the life-energy of the soul. As the soul 'descends from grace' it shrouds itself in veils of matter which serve to shield it from the divine gaze we know as the love of God.

Those who manifest as physical beings experience the reality of the 'spacious present' as the phenomenon of space-time. Within the 'spacious present' this manifestation of life is simultaneous and all lives are coexistent, but to the incarnate soul these lives are separated in time and space. As the soul 'ascends' to the realisation of its divine being the veils are progressively cast aside and the revelation unfolds before its very eyes. At the 'at-one-ment' on the plane of the soul the Ascension is complete, but in the 'spacious present' there is no beginning or ending.

With respect to Mrs. G's letter, I would stress that we need to be careful how we use our terms. Focusing, by definition, is an activity which requires a focal point. To talk about a 'spirit' focusing in more than one place at a time is a contradiction in terms. If a spirit could focus in more than one place at a time it could focus in twenty places or even a million of places at a time, indeed everywhere. This is the exact opposite of the meaning of the word 'focus'. I will indicate, below, that Mrs. G's observations refer to the spiritual activities of the Group Soul. We note, in passing, that elevated spirit communicators always form part of a group.

I disagree with Mrs. G's remark that we are wasting our precious energy discussing 'time' issues beyond the physical. Although we can hardly imagine the freedom of the 'spacious present' from the limitations of space-time, we can certainly establish logical relations between the two. The relationship is, essentially, a mathematical one and corresponds to the 'sequential' and the 'simultaneous'.

With respect to T.S's observations, I would emphasize that bodies (physical, etheric, astral, mental etc.) are not souls but manifestations of the soul. The whole variety of psychic or mediumistic phenomena we call possession, obsession, bi-location, astral projection, community of sensation, clairvoyance etc. are, merely excursions by the various bodies functioning as 'interfaces' between the soul and the planes of matter. The claim that my conclusions are unsupported by the scriptures and by clairvoyant and other investigations is interesting. Could I please be supplied with chapter and verse?

I agree, completely, that several souls may share one physical body. This is a very important observation. On the question of Hindu occultism, I find it unsurprising that a believer in reincarnation would interpret 'past life' material as evidence in favour of reincarnation. Visions of past lives by 'seers' can be understood, more readily, as manifestations or incarnations of the Group Soul.

Incarnation is an activity of the Group Soul. Perhaps the easiest way to describe this is to use the 'hand in glove' analogy. The hand represents the Group Soul and the fingers represent each member of the group. The glove represents the 'body of manifestation'. Each finger of the glove 'points' to a region in space-time as the field of endeavour for the incarnating soul. Normally the glove fits perfectly and every member of the group incarnates in only one body. However, other situations are possible. Two or more fingers may fit (albeit uncomfortably) into 'one' hole of the glove i.e. two or more souls may share the same body. Finally some fingers may not fit into any holes at all. In this case the lives would be 'aborted' and the bodies rejected. Clearly one finger cannot fit into more than one hole of the glove simultaneously. Under this analogy one soul cannot incarnate in more than one body. In this paradigm reincarnation is meaningless.

Clearly, the result hinges on the 'hand-in-glove' analogy. The key word, implicit in the proof, is 'focus'. One or more souls may focus their attention in one body but one soul cannot focus his or her attention in more than one body. This would be a contradiction in terms. In the language of mathematics we would say that incarnation is a 'one-to-one', 'many-to-one' correspondence from souls to bodies. Reincarnation, however, is a 'one-to-many', 'many-to-many' correspondence. In this case a soul could, miraculously, occupy more than one body at a time. It would be like trying to fit a single finger into two or more holes of the glove simultaneously. I maintain that the 'one-to-one', 'many-to-one' rule is a fundamental law of human incarnation.

It is interesting to note, in passing, that this 'one-to-one' 'many-to-one' rule describes the great body of 'well-behaved' functions in mathematics and physics. Without them the theory and practice of science at the human level would be impossible. An experiment would always have more than one outcome even if the initial conditions were unchanged. Imagine walking upstairs and finding that they had disappeared on the way down! Fortunately nature works rationally and according to law.

However there is a more fundamental objection to the doctrine of reincarnation. In the universe there is a deep principle at work which can be called the Law of Economy. It means that the physical universe runs on 'minimum energy' principles. It is why, for example, the surface area of a soap bubble is minimized to form a perfect sphere. We know that matter and energy are interchangeable ($E = mc^2$) and that physical bodies are forms of energy. Given the number of incarnating souls, the 'minimum energy principle' requires that the number of physical bodies (energy) be minimised. The phenomenon of 'body sharing' by several souls is the best evidence we have that human incarnation is governed by this principle. At the same time it confirms that the minimum number of physical bodies is established at a figure below the number of incarnating souls. It suggests, very strongly, the pressure to incarnate on earth is greater than the planet's resources. In other words Nature economizes. She allows two or more souls to share the same body but prohibits one soul from utilizing more than one body. Hence the number of physical bodies may not exceed the number of incarnating souls. This confirms the 'one-to-one', 'many-to-one' rule of human incarnation.

The Law of Economy is universal. In the physical universe it is the 'principle of minimum energy'. In the spiritual universe it is the 'principle of harmony'. The Law must be obeyed throughout the physical and spiritual universes. It is inviolable.

Reincarnation violates the 'minimum energy principle' because it fails to minimize the number of physical bodies (energy). Indeed the number of physical bodies would be limitless. An incarnate soul could extend, indefinitely, the number of his or her physical lives by refusing to progress – there is no automatic mechanism of release for errant souls. In the language of mathematics we would say that the solution is 'unbounded'. Fortunately the 'minimum energy principle' debars the return of wayward souls to the physical, though many do remain earth-bound to exercise a malign influence on those still living on earth. However the 'principle of harmony' comes into play and, eventually, they are drawn towards the Light. The two principles work in harmony. The Law of Economy is universal.

We have to conclude that the doctrine of reincarnation is, indeed, a fallacy. Although my arguments have been presented informally, they embody a mathematical theorem. This theorem may be expressed as follows:

Human incarnation is a 'one-to-one', 'many-to-one' correspondence from souls to physical bodies.

Yours sincerely,
Steve Blake M.Sc.(Lond.)

On the 13th. January 2004 Steve wrote another fine letter to *Psychic World* which unfortunately was not published. Newspapers do tend to call a halt, often just as the debate gets warmed up, on any particular subject. This is probably because a wider ongoing tendency has to be maintained for the sake of the readership. Obviously I cannot comment as to reason why.

I feel it would be important for the readers if I mention and quote from Steve's letter his responses to comments previously made from two particular readers of *Psychic World* and then conclude with a fine paper which summarises the principle points he had established.

The Editor
Psychic World

Dear Mr. Taylor

With regard to *D.O's* comments on the Group Soul, we must avoid confusion. The Group Soul in humanity has meaning only when groups of human souls feel spiritually 'close' to one another. It is experienced as spiritual affinity and realised through common purpose and destiny. The Group Soul is, therefore, a subjective experience between souls and cannot be observed, measured or delimited. Souls who are spiritually 'close' to one another often incarnate as a group of physical beings. Some may incarnate as contemporaries, belonging to the same family or social group, others may incarnate in different historical time periods. At a deep level the problems and challenges experienced by one soul are available to all other members of the group and, ultimately, to all members of the human family. The Group Soul concept accounts for a number of phenomena: memories of 'past lives', multiple personalities. aborted lives, conjoined twins, special affinity between groups of people. It should be stressed, however, that the logic of incarnation does not depend on the Group Soul concept. If there were no group souls the law of incarnation would still apply. Using the 'hand-in-glove' analogy in which fingers correspond to physical bodies (see my previous letter November 2003), the absence of Group Souls would simply mean that the 'body of manifestation' would be one large 'glove' with many fingers instead of many smaller 'gloves' with fewer fingers.

D.O's argument that the Law of Economy cannot be applied to *numbers* of bodies because number has no mass or extension in space is incorrect. The Law of Economy, as the 'minimum energy principle', is applicable to anything which can be quantified. The only mathematical difference between say the *mass* of a body and the *number* of bodies is that, in this particular case, mass is a 'continuous' variable and number is a 'discrete' variable. Examples of continuous variables would be mass, energy, volume of water in a tank, quantity of fabric on a roll; discrete variables would be the number of people in a football stadium, the number of sweets in a jar, the number of flowers in a vase. To show that the 'minimum energy principle' applies to both the *mass* of bodies and the *number* of bodies I shall use a simple example. Let us suppose that a manufacturer is required to produce five hundred pairs of gloves subject to the condition that each glove *must* have at least five fingers and that each glove *must fit* onto the hand however loosely. If the quantity of material and resources available to the manufacturer is *unlimited* then all kinds of unusual design configurations are possible. Gloves with arbitrary number of fingers, in any quantity and size could be produced. Clearly the solution to the problem would be 'unbounded'. However the Law of Economy requires that the quantity of material used by the manufacturer be minimized; but also the *number* of fingers in each glove would be equal to five. Clearly the problem has a solution. If in place of 'quantity of material' we read 'mass' and in place of 'fingers' we read 'physical bodies' then the 'minimum energy principle' minimizes both the mass and the *number* of physical bodies.

With regard to M.E's comments, his assertion that 'Nature's system is effective but not economical' is a view which has been propounded by evolutionists. According to this view Nature uses a random mechanism to produce new forms and, under environmental pressures and competition, only 'successful' ones are selected. Since many forms are rejected, or become extinct in the process of natural selection, the implied wastage is enormous.

Firstly I would point out that the theory of evolution has *never* been supported by the fossil record. After 150 years of intensive digging and excavation the enormous number of intermediate forms, required by the theory, have never been found. If Charles Darwin were alive today he would, most likely, reject the theory of evolution as being unsupported by the evidence. With regard to Michael's 'acorn tree' example I would say that the idea of an 'acorn tree' is, actually, an artificial division or 'system' imposed by naturalists on a small aspect of the natural world for the purposes of study and research. In reality the natural world is an organic whole and knows no boundaries. What we 'see' as an organism is a part of a whole. A leaf is a part of a branch, a branch is part of a tree, a tree is part of a forest, and so on until the whole biosphere is embraced. To assert that an 'acorn tree' is uneconomical or wasteful with acorns is as meaningless as it is to assert that a branch is uneconomical with leaves or that a forest is uneconomical with trees. In reality what appears to be 'wasted' by one organism can be used with benefit by another organism. If the system around the 'acorn tree' is extended to encompass a wider area of study and research, the apparent 'wastage' is contained within the system and the 'acorn tree' appears to be an element of a wider network of organic and inorganic relationships. In a closed system the Law of Conservation of Energy ensures that one form of energy is, merely, converted to another form – the total amount of energy remains constant and nothing is lost. The concept of 'wastage' in Nature is no more than a human prejudice or value judgement.

Incidently the Law of Conservation of Energy is another physical manifestation of the Law of Economy.

Michael's information about spirit views on reincarnation is interesting. The problem with accepting spirit communications as authoritative is that, taken as a whole, they are often contradictory – especially where reincarnation is concerned. Ultimately the recipients of such information choose who and what they want to believe. We need to recognise that when we 'kick off' the physical 'garment' and awaken to the spiritual life we retain our sincerely held beliefs, opinions *and* prejudices. From our point of view it can take 'ages' before spirits fully awaken to their true condition. A scientist of repute when on earth becomes no automatic authority on spiritual matters in the next life – especially if he or she were a materialist. Spirits who communicate the 'truth' of reincarnation are merely conveying their own beliefs acquired on earth. Although 'spirit groups' usually set their own agenda and communicate with us in their own time, I would make the following suggestion:

Any spirit who professes a belief in reincarnation should be presented with a 'proof' that reincarnation is impossible.

In a different context Carl Wickland (*Thirty Years Among the Dead*) reasoned with 'earthbound' spirits until they 'saw the light'. Spirits who are still wedded to earthly obsessions and beliefs would be well-advised to 'focus' more on the spiritual and less on the physical.

Yours sincerely
Steve Blake, M.Sc.(Lond.)

A FORMAL REFUTATION OF THE DOCTRINE OF REINCARNATION
Steve Blake M.Sc. (Lond.)

Introduction and Summary

The formal refutation is contained in a number of propositions which show that the doctrine of reincarnation is logically incompatible with the idea of human immortality. In other words reincarnation and human immortality cannot *both* be true. The proof is based upon two fundamental axioms and a principle which relates the *temporal* to the *eternal* (see below). The main result is:

Proposition 7: No *human soul incarnates more than once*

This proposition may surprise many people, especially those who are committed to the idea of reincarnation, and might well provoke the jibe that a thousand million Buddhists and Hindus cannot all be wrong! However this is beside the point. Buddhism and Hinduism have never taught the Western concept of human immortality so it would be self-defeating to appeal to these religions for support. I shall not enter into a lengthy discussion of Eastern metaphysics but quote from an authoritative source:

A Handbook of Living Religions - John R. Hinnells (ed).

In the case of Hinduism:

'Shankara asserted that only Brahman was real, all else, including the phenomenal world, the sense of individuality, even the devas, was unreal ... When the human spirit, through meditation and enlightenment, realizes that it is itself of the substance of Brahman and has no separate identity, then it merges with Brahman, as the drop is absorbed in the ocean'. (p.207)

In the case of Buddhism:

'Buddhism is a middle way between eternalism (belief in personal immortality) and annihilation (belief that death is the final end). If eternalism is a rigid view (*ditthi*), motivated by craving and obstructing the path to liberation, it is counterproductive to describe the goal as if it were some permanent state of being'. (p.307)

It should be clear that the goal of both religions is the 'liberation' of the self from human or spiritual identity. In Hinduism individual consciousness is ultimately absorbed into an ocean of consciousness (*moksha*). In Buddhism individual consciousness is eventually 'snuffed out' like the flame of a candle (*nirvana*). *Moksha* and *nirvana* both represent states of being in which human individuality has no meaning or reality. In the language of Western thought this is to assert that the human soul is mortal and must ultimately perish.

It is surely no coincidence that the two major religions which propound the doctrine of reincarnation *also* teach that the human soul is mortal. This aspect of reincarnationism has been carefully concealed from Western devotees beneath an edifice of quasi-spiritual thought designed primarily to fascinate rather than educate. Many spiritualists who believe in reincarnation are completely unaware that this is the case and persistently appeal to these religions in support of their beliefs.

This result is expressed in the following proposition:

Proposition 8: Reincarnation implies that the human soul is mortal

Since my main interest lies in mathematical and logical structures I prefer to express the key result (Proposition 7) in mathematical form. Human incarnation can then be regarded as a mathematical correspondence between souls and physical bodies. It is summed up in what I have called the Law of Human Incarnation:

Human incarnation is a one-to-one, many-to-one correspondence from souls to physical bodies

The axioms, on which this result is based, are fundamental to our concepts of individuality, human responsibility and immortality. If we accept the basic premises of the argument then the law is proven.

The relevance of this law to the spiritualist movement is clear. Those spiritualists (and spirit communicators) who propound the doctrine of reincarnation *and* human immortality are teaching two mutually contradictory ideas – like teaching that the earth is both universally 'flat' *and* 'spheroidal'. Reincarnation is not a matter of choice or compulsion for the human soul. If it is understood that the human soul *is* immortal then reincarnation becomes a meaningless concept.

THE FORMAL REFUTATION

As stated above the refutation is based upon two fundamental axioms and a principle which relates the temporal to the eternal.

The Reduction Principle: The temporal to the eternal is relatively null

This principle lays down the fundamental relationship between the temporal and the eternal. The temporal is a transient, material, space-time domain of finite potential. The eternal is a permanent, spaceless, timeless domain of pure consciousness and infinite unfolding potential. Compared to eternity, space-time has no permanent reality i.e. duration is relatively zero and physical space is perceived as a single dimensionless point. In other words space-time is relatively null. In mathematical terms the temporal and the eternal can be treated as a polarity between the finite and the infinite. The Reduction Principle gives us the following simple but fundamental equation:

$$\text{time/eternity} = \text{zero}$$

Axiom 1: Every human soul is immortal.

This axiom can be accepted with or without proof, or deduced from more fundamental axioms involving belief in God. For the purpose of this proof it is not necessary to define the nature of the human soul. We need only accept that the human soul is immortal.

Axiom 2: Different people have different souls.

The second axiom is the foundation of human individuality. It assigns spiritual and moral responsibility to each human being living on earth. Normally a human being has only one soul. However it is perfectly consistent with the idea of 'multiple possession'. The key idea is that however many souls may be associated with one human body they *must* be different to the souls associated with another human body. This axiom lays down the fundamental relationship between mortal and immortal life.

Let us see what may be deduced from these axioms.

Proposition 1: Every human soul is unique.
Proof: By Axiom 1 every human soul is immortal and, therefore, eternal. Since all human souls are eternal they are coexistent. If they are coexistent they must be different and, therefore, unique.

Proposition 2: The temporal and the eternal form a polarity corresponding to human mortality in time and human immortality in eternity.
Proof: We know that human souls express themselves as human beings in time and space. Furthermore we know that the human body is mortal (or perishable) and, by Axiom 1, that every human soul is immortal (or imperishable). Thus human mortality is a phenomenon of the temporal but human *immortality* is a reality of the eternal.

Proposition 3: To eternity duration is zero and all events are simultaneous.
Proof: By the Reduction Principle duration is relatively zero i.e. (time/eternity) = zero. It follows immediately that, in comparison with eternity, the *interval* between two instants of time is also zero i.e. (time interval/eternity) = zero. Since all temporal events can be assigned dates then all dates and events must be relatively simultaneous. This proves the third proposition.

Proposition 4: To eternity the creation and incarnation of human souls are simultaneous events.
Proof: This is an immediate corollary of Proposition 3.

Proposition 5: All contemporaneous human beings living in time and space have different souls.

Proof: By Axiom 2, different people have different souls. Thus the soul(s) associated with one human body must be *different* to the soul(s) associated with another human body. If this were not true then a number of human beings living and working at the same time would be sharing the same soul(s). This would be a denial of human individuality and in conflict with Axiom 2. Hence the proposition is proven.

Proposition 6: All non-contemporaneous human beings living in time and space have different souls.
Proof: To eternity all events are simultaneous (Proposition 3). This means that the lives of all human beings past, present, and future, from the eternal point of view, are simultaneous events. This is merely to say that, to eternity, all human beings living in time and space lead contemporaneous lives. From Proposition 5 we have, therefore, proven Proposition 6.

Proposition 7: No human soul incarnates more than once.
Proof: We prove this proposition by the method of contradiction. Let us suppose that a human soul *does* incarnate more than once. More specifically suppose soul S incarnates as human beings H_1 H_2 H_3 H_4 H_5 in different historical time periods. In this case there would be several human beings associated with only one soul S. This contradicts Proposition 5 and 6 which require that all human beings living in time and space have different souls. Therefore our initial supposition that a human soul incarnates more than once is *false*. This proves the proposition.

Proposition 8: Reincarnation implies that the human soul is mortal.

Proof: By Axiom 1, every human soul is immortal, and by proposition 7 no human soul incarnates more than once. It follows, immediately, if an entity *does* incarnate more than once, then it cannot be an immortal human soul. In the reincarnating paradigm a human soul who incarnates more than once cannot be immortal. (If it *was* immortal it would not reincarnate - by Axiom 1 and proposition 7). Conversely a reincarnating entity who is immortal cannot be a human soul. The first case establishes proposition 8.

To summarize, we have shown that if the doctrine of reincarnation is true then the human soul is mortal and must, ultimately, perish. In this sense the doctrine of reincarnation is a variant of 'materialism'. In the case of 'materialism' the human soul (if there is one) perishes at the first dissolution of the physical body. In the case of 'reincarnationism' the human soul perishes following a finite sequence of incarnations.

We arrive at the fundamental Law of Human Incarnation:

Proposition 9: Human incarnation is a one-to-one, many-to-one correspondence from souls to physical bodies

CHAPTER 12

From Both Sides of the Pond
John Gillespie – Alan Ross

I began corresponding with John Gillespie fairly recently when we discovered that our views were very much in common. He has become a colleague and granted me permission to quote from his work for which I am most grateful.

John is a family man, married with two children and lives in Wiltshire. He has an interesting and well quali- fied background, mainly engineering – ScoTEC Mechan- ical and Production Eng. (1981); BTEC Microprocessor Eng. (1986); B.Sc. Science and Technology (Open 1998); M.Sc. in Science (Open 2001); PGCE (BSUC 2002).

He is also interested in spiritual matters including the occult, science and world religions and is a member of the SNU (Spiritualists' National Union).

John Gillespie's present occupation is as a science master teaching 11 to 18 year old pupils.

I would like to quote from John's letters and articles published in *Psychic World* in August and October 2005. Minor editing (mine) and any alterations or additions by John have been mutually agreed and approved:

..............The next point that needs to be discussed is with respect to 'past lives', reincarnation and regression. Here I find it incredulous that many Spiritualists believe in reincarnation and the existence in past lives without the slightest thought to other possible explanations.

Even though I personally do not believe in reincarnation, it cannot be denied the facts provided by 'regressed' people are often exceptional in both accuracy, quality and quantity. So from a scientific perspective this alone indicates the presence of a background medium of some kind, as either there has been a real 'rebirth' of a formerly deceased intelligence into another body, or the person believing they have lived before has tapped into a 'universal consciousness permeating space and time'. Both explanations are beyond the knowledge of conventional science and as such should be explored. Now back to my original point. As a non-believer in reincarnation I would like to provide some information that should help others formulate their own opinions on this subject.

The first example of an alternative to reincarnation describes a research project where unsuspecting students were, over an extended period, subjected to subliminal messages, such as overhearing deliberate conversations about alien abduction. Then when under hypnosis many of these subjects provided highly convincing and detailed 'false' memories. The recalled memories were completely induced. Other examples of false memory syndrome focus on the influence of the media on our subconscious memory, and the unintentional steering of a regressed individual to give answers that the regressing hypnotist wants, but without consciously being aware they are doing it. (Prof. Carl Sagan, 1997. *The Demon-Haunted*

World; Prof. Ellison, *Science and the Paranormal*; also see the work of psychologist Dr. Susan Blackmore).

Dr. Melvin Morse (Morse, 2000. *Where God Lives*) gives an example where two children, alive at the same time, recount the same past life even from thousands of miles apart in the USA. Morse puts this coincident phenomena down, not to past lives but to the children linking into a 'memory bank', a universal repository of all the memories accumulated from past lives (sounds a bit Jungian?).

Another alternative and one that many Spiritualists have witnessed is that of trance mediumship. Many of us have seen a medium induce a self hypnotic trance state for the purpose of communicating with discarnate spirits. The medium is often able to produce remarkable 'verifiable' evidence from a bygone age, an age where the communicating spirit lived their mortal life prior to death. This scenario is not dissimilar to that of a 'regressed' trance like state and a discarnate spirit communicating through an unsuspecting 'hypnotised' individual, although to them it is evidence of their past life and not their channelling the memories of a departed spirit.

I would like to further suggest a possible alternative to the claims where regression has been used successfully to cure phobias, phobias suggested to be residue from a previous incarnated life. If, as is often suggested, children are generally very aware of the presence of discarnate spirits, even to the point of obsessive or schizophrenic tendencies, then maybe as a child we may be able to form a strong attachment with a discarnate spirit, or many spirits as in the latter case, where fears or pre-death experiences are impinging on the conscious/subconscious of the developing child causing it to have fears, and ultimately phobias that have no causal connection to their present childhood experiences. Then we could consider the possibility of the regressing hypnotist, when clearing the phobia, is in fact performing a 'spirit' rescue releasing any 'attached' spirit, or spirits. Once the spirit influence has been removed the phobia is also removed, the person is outwardly cured and attributes the miraculous change to a hang-up from a previous incarnation. Incorrectly believing he or she had reincarnated.

It is also not beyond the realms of possibility, that as a foetus develops in the womb, a discarnate spirit may influence its growth and produce strategic birthmarks. This may be controversial and I feel certain that many who read this will object, however we know spirit can produce physical phenomena so why not cause birthmarks to match the marks left by injuries sustained by discarnate spirit prior to its death.

I have read many accounts of reincarnation, and met many people in the UK who believe they remember past lives. I have also met a senior member of the SNU who advertises the fact they carry out past life regressions, a service they have conducted for over thirty years. When confronted on the validity of what they professed as fact, and even though given alternatives to the notion of the existence of past lives, they refused to accept any other consideration and argued that they knew regression was fact purely on the grounds they had been doing it for thirty or so years. Unfortunately the mere fact you do something for thirty years is not justification for regression being a real phenomena! I could argue that the Earth is the centre of the Universe – or flat – for thirty years, but it still does not mean I am right – just ignorant of all the facts!

Just because someone does something such as regression for thirty years, getting a wealth of evidence of what may at first appear as past lives, has no validity when viewed under the empiricist's microscope, and as such does not constitute evidence to support the case for reincarnation..........

John Gillespie followed up with a further response from which I quote these extracts:

..................For those who did not read August's issue of *Psychic World*, I suggested, along with supporting evidence, that past life regression may not be evidential as proof of reincarnation on the grounds that it could be unconscious mediumship, or false memory. That is to say the regressed mind is enabled, similar to a medium in trance, to tap into the consciousness of departed souls within the unseen dimension of life – that which is commonly referred to as the 'spirit world' – or made to recall unconscious 'false' memories. I further suggested that phobias and strategic birthmarks that correspond with supposed aspects of a prior incarnate existence, are the result of something close to a possession, where a discarnate spirit has made a very close psycho-physical connection to the living and growing individual, influencing their mortal life. A connection which the individual is totally unaware of except for certain unexplained phobias or other psychological problems.

It is not beyond the realms of possibility that schizophrenia, multiple personality disorder and other such psychological conditions may have their pathology linked to such 'discarnate spirit' influences.

I can appreciate Estelle's argument in respect to reincarnation and can only reaffirm my previous comments that it matters little how long you do something, time does not make it true. We have a multitude of examples throughout history where certain things were held as the truth purely because people knew no better, or were bound by deep seated religious conviction. The examples given in the original letter were the *Geocentric (or Earth Centred) Universe*, and *Flat Earth*, both totally wrong and both defended with dire consequences for those who spoke against them. Yet no matter how long these ideas were defended it did not, and still does not make them true!

Just because someone experiences, or carries out past-life regressions for thirty years means absolutely nothing.

The notion of Karma as a supporting case for reincarnation has its basis in ancient lore. How can a society maintain civil order unless it has something to threaten the ignorant and potentially anarchic masses. Do not forget that education, in the Western world at least, has not always been available to all. In fact, until the past few hundred years or so, the only people who were educated were either rich, and those pursuing a life in priesthood.

To maintain order we have laws, laws that set out what you must, or must not do. These laws, irrespective of your cultural or religious bias, are similar to the Christian Ten Commandments and Spiritualism's Seven Principles. Karma is just an extension of early law whereby if you do wrong you will have to pay it back either in this life, or in your next incarnation. In Christianity if you do wrong you will be judged then head for hell-fire and damnation, and not an everlasting life in heaven – a similar fate awaits naughty Moslems – and one should not forget either, Spiritualism's *Compensation and Retribution...*(the 6th principle) where once again we must face our misdeeds.

We need to get things in perspective and first consider 'time'. Modern human beings have been evolving on this planet for some forty thousand years, that's 40,000 years to learn not to steal, not to kill, in fact not to do any deed that will cause civil unrest among our fellows. Our ancestors realised that in order to maintain a social structure where we could move around without fear of being killed, or having our possessions stolen, there had to be some way to get the populous to behave in a civilised manner, and avoid anarchic chaos. Hence we have religions or social rules (laws) to maintain order. Here I will add that religion is purely a means to control the minds of the masses through the addition of divine intervention, if you sin or offend God you will suffer untold agonies, or similar fate.

Much of the religious writings purportedly from God are mythological relics composed into books by priests to gain obedience through fear.

Reincarnation and karma are examples of another mechanism of control. They are psychological tools designed to get members of a developing society to comply with acceptable social order. For example, if a person considers killing another, and if they believe in karma, they may reconsider doing the act because of the implications it will have in this life and for their next incarnation (i.e. return as a slave, or worse, to repay their debt to the person they killed).

Spiritualism has a similar behaviour control within its 5th and 6th Principles where it suggests that not only are we personally responsibly for all our actions, we will have to pay the price for any transgressions in the here and hereafter. This may suggest the possibility of reincarnation although the Principle in question just states hereafter, where hereafter could be any post-mortem existence other than that of this physical world.

In conclusion may I say this: Many Spiritualists sit back and ingest every idea given as though it were a fact, as exemplified by reincarnation, past lives and karma. We really do not know if past lives are a fact, and we cannot just accept it on the basis of 'time served anec-dotes'. As I have suggested, there are numerous other explanations to account for the phenomena. Even karma, which is an early expression of *cause and effect*, once again cannot be verified based on coincidences and anec-dotes.......

.......Whatever you did in a previous existence (if such a thing is possible) is not important unless to feed the ego of the individual. Also is it possible that it is easier for the ego to believe its psychological hang-ups are residue from a past life than to believe they are influ-ences from an unknown external spirit intelligence. Past-lifer's do you really know the difference?

—⁓—

And now to the other side of the pond, to America, where another friend and colleague is Alan Ross who resides in Florida, U.S.A. He wrote a book *Spiritualism*

And Beyond which amongst the interesting contents includes an important chapter on Reincarnation.

Alan points out that reincarnation is not officially a part of Spiritualism but admits that for sometime he did believe in it but that he no longer did, and then went on to relate his experiences that brought him to this conclusion. I do not have space enough to detail these in my book, as I would like, but would advise readers to refer to Alan's book. Nevertheless, I must mention Alan's visit to the Spiritualist community in Western New York State called Lily Dale, established in 1879, not far from the birth place of Modern Spiritualism. It is a community of mediums where communication with spirits is demonstrated and healing is offered. I quote Alan's words:

.......While there, I was fortunate to meet with the president of the Association, Rev. Joseph H. Merrill. To my surprise he informed me that he was a non-reincarnationist, as were a majority of the other board members. Rev. Merrill was so certain of his belief that he had written a small booklet aptly titled *Do I Have To Return?* ....

Rev. Merrill writes in his book how spirits are continually interacting with the mortal world. Child prodigies and child geniuses are said to be old souls who have come back in rebirth. Do people not know that children are most susceptible to spirit influence from birth to six or seven years of age, whether that influencing spirit is a musician, mathematician, poet or writer of prose? How easy it is to forget that spirits are around us at all times, mingling and co-mingling.

Alan then later goes on to say:

......While exploring the Lily Dale library, I discovered, *The History of Spiritualism* by Sir Arthur Conan Doyle, author of the Sherlock Holmes mystery novels. In it Sir Arthur writes, '*If reincarnation were true, there must have been millions of spiritualists, who, upon entering the other world, have sought in vain their kindred, children and friends. Has one whisper of such a woe ever reached us from the thousands of communicating spirits? Never!*'

I thought how ridiculous it would be to hear a medium from the platform say, '*I am sorry dear, but your mom can't be here to greet you this evening because she has taken another body and is back on the earth.*' Neither I nor anyone I know has ever heard anything like that, and the reason is because they are all there. If reincarnation were true, it would mean no joyous reunion with loved ones because everyone would be popping up and down from one world to the other.

I would like to quote here the important remarks Alan Ross made in his conclusion to the chapter:

I believe that people embrace reincarnation because it is a far better alternative than purgatory or hell. I also believe that people feel comfortable with the idea of returning to the familiarity of the earth – the only home they have ever known. I am convinced that the earth is a mere *way station* on the soul's eternal journey from a formless entity to a perfected spirit. In this process the soul does not retrace its steps or method of existence, it will not go from being a spirit back to being a mortal. When mortals die, their souls have already achieved the purpose of their incarnation, that is, the individualization of the soul. A soul may become purified through the exercise of will and the expression of remorse in the spirit world. It is, therefore, not necessary for the spirit to go back to the flesh for more chances to purify itself.

I realize, for many people, the idea that reincarnation will not be the destiny of their soul may be disappointing and difficult to accept. They may think that they will not be able to shed their karma if they cannot return to the earth to do it. I am convinced, however, to the contrary – that it is far easier and more merciful to achieve perfection in the spirit world without the encumbrance of the physical body and the burden of a countless succession of earth lives.

I now have complete faith in a great spiritual world filled with billions of spirits progressing toward wonders that, for now are beyond our conception, a world created for the eternal existence of the soul and one that contains the knowledge and wisdom of the ages. If people could only realize the happiness that awaits them, they would not be attached to returning to the earth, but would instead strive to progress through the spheres of consciousness towards the fountainhead of the spiritual light of God.

CHAPTER 13

Reincarnation or
Ray-Incarnation?

**Charlotte Waterlow MA., MBE. (1915 -)
and Lawrence Hyde (1896-1958)**

Charlotte Waterlow lives in Gloucestershire. I have
known her for many years and quite recently have
enjoyed a number of telephone conversations and corre-
spondences with her, regarding my book, and requesting
the privilege of including some extracts from her writings, particularly on the subject of reincarnation. That
permission has been duly given.

Introduction:

*Charlotte Waterlow was born in England, the daughter
of a diplomat, in 1915. She graduated from Cambridge
University with first class honours in History in 1936
and has had an active career, working in the British
Foreign Office (1945-53) and then, until her retirement
in 1982, she taught modern world history at the senior
level, first in a girls' Grammar School at Guildford,
England, then at a private Co-educational High School
in Cambridge, Massachusetts, USA. She is the author of*

four text books dealing with 20th century history and contemporary affairs. At the age of twenty she was launched into spiritual philosophy by Lawrence Hyde, who she regarded as her 'mentor', and its insights have informed all her work. She has more recently written 'The Hinge of History' (published 1995 by The One World Trust) which discusses past, present and future in terms of the evolution of consciousness.

Here is a quote from 'The Hinge of History' (Chapter 3 *Religion and Philosophy* page 32):

The Eastern religions are therefore essentially religions of method, inculcating meditation, yoga practices and good works. The great Hindu Gods, and the Buddha, are held up as *models*. A major teaching is that of reincarnation. Everyone is responsible for his/her own deeds and development – this is the doctrine of *karma*. But one short human life is not normally sufficient for the necessary experiences for personal growth or for the putting right of wrongs done. Only when, after a series of incarnations, perhaps over a period of centuries, has the individual gained enlightenment, is he or she free from 'the wheel of rebirth' and able to dwell in states of glory. He may then return to earth as an Enlightened One, a Hindu *Avatar*, or a Buddha, to help to redeem and uplift humankind.

To me, the weakness of this doctrine, as it applies to ordinary people here and now, is its narcissism. It does not provide for redemption by love in ordinary life. If I, a modern high school teacher, *am* the Pharaoh Akhenaten, the latter has not progressed very far since he died over 3,000 years ago! But if I – and probably many others – are 'overshadowed' by Akhenaten, now a god-like soul, the situation is very different. For love flows between the overshadower and the overshadowee – however unconscious the latter may be of the fact; and this love, expressed in unions of groups as well as of individuals, transmutes the evil deeds of the past and provides the spiritual energies to build the future.

Bearing each the others' burdens, sharing each the others' joys, between souls incarnate and discarnate, is the heretical Waterlow version of the doctrines of reincarnation and of karma.

—⁊⁊⁊—

I am including extracts from Charlotte Waterlow's abridged and edited version of an original book by Lawrence Hyde – *The Mystery of Karma .... Reincarnation or Ray-Incarnation?* which was published as a booklet by the Kosmon Church for whom I acknowledge credit and permission to copy from.

Charlotte Waterlow was the author of the first chapter and so I will begin by quoting from that chapter:

It is natural that a great many people who are responsive to the spiritual currents of the New Age should turn to the ancient doctrine of reincarnation, taught in particular by Hinduism and Buddhism, and by some of the ancient Greeks. According to this doctrine, each person's karma is worked out through a series of rebirths in a physical body; this process continues until the soul has achieved full expression of its archetypal nature; then it is released from 'The Wheel of Rebirth', to return finally to its celestial home.

The doctrine of Reincarnation is flowing today like a stream of thirst-quenching water into minds and hearts parched by the arid psychological climate of our secular society. It offers an explanation of suffering, and hope of redemption and creative fulfilment which is very romantic and apparently very rational, but in its popular form, at least, it has certain basic limitations. First, it does not provide adequately for the evolution of the soul after death. If after 3,000 years in 'the other world' that ancient Egyptian priestess is just that ordinary person, 'me', then she has not evolved very far! Second, if she is <u>me</u>, and I am identifying with <u>myself</u> when I identify with her, then a fundamentally narcissistic situation arises, with all its attendant psychological dangers. Third, the reincarnationist is cut off from communion with the vast world of discarnate souls, ranging from the god-like to the diabolic, which modern spiritualism is opening up. He is thrown back into the physical world when his consciousness should be expanding objectively in far wider realms. Finally, the doctrine is statistically absurd, since there are far more people alive today (at least six billion by the end of the 20th century) than have ever lived in the world's history, so they cannot all be reincarnations!

There is, however, a 'deeper' version of the orthodox doctrine, which may be called the concept of Ray or Group Incarnation. It asserts that after death the individual soul does not reincarnate, but evolves through many spiritual states, developing his potentialities ever more fully until he finally becomes 'god-like'. During this evolutionary process he draws near to the earth plane from time to time, assuming a suitable dense 'etheric body', like a person putting on a suitable suit of clothes, in order to 'overshadow' his spiritual descendants, to whom he is bound by karmic ties. Through this communion of souls the person on earth receives spiritual illumination and strength to carry on the work of the spiritual ancestors, to promote the welfare of the world, and to put right the wrongs which the ancestors committed. The collective karma of the spiritual family is thus worked out through the great principle of redemption through love. Many of us experience, some time in our lives, communion (as distinct from communication) with another human being, perhaps with several human beings, at what may be called the soul level; and we find that this is bliss – it brings a deeper sense of reality than can ever be found through physical contact, mental communication or emotional passion. Imagine the bliss of communion with discarnate souls of exalted spiritual stature! 'Where two or three are gathered together, there I am'. For love at the soul level attuned all lovers to the cosmos, 'the ordered harmony of the universe', as the Greek philosophers saw it. And this love is in its nature redemptive. Thus through 'communion with angels', and with human affinities, a person finds his place in the karmic web of relationships, in the process of spiritual evolution which is working itself out through the interweaving groups which comprise the cosmopolis, the universal community of men and gods. The doctrine of Ray Incarnation is thus in essence a lofty form of spiritualism.

Particularly in the Hindu and Buddhist religions, the great classic doctrine of Reincarnation has emerged to explain the progress of the soul towards its full development and 'emancipation' from the world of illusion. When this doctrine infiltrated into the West in the 19th century, therefore, it fell on fertile ground. It came partly through the Oriental scriptures, which were being discovered, translated and edited by Western scholars, and partly through individuals who visited the East, where they easily absorbed it and formulated it into a Western system of thought. The most famous and influential of these systems was that of the Theosophical Society, founded by the Russian seer H.P. Blavatsky. The Theosophical system will therefore be taken as the basis for our critique of the doctrine.

—⟋⟍—

..................At this point it would be appropriate to provide the reader with a background of Lawrence Hyde and then proceed with the extracts:

LAWRENCE HYDE (1896-1958) served as a pilot in World War 1, and then gained a diploma in anthropology at Oxford University. In World War II he worked in London as translator for the exiled President of Benes of Czechoslovakia. He was also for a time editor of 'Light', the Journal of the College of Psychic Science in London. He devoted the main part of his life to the study of spiritual philosophy, publishing seven books* in this field and leaving behind him four unpublished manuscripts now in the possession of Charlotte Waterlow. 'The Nameless Faith' (Rider 1949), probably his best book, is dedicated to: *Those in all lands who are inspired by the ideal of a 'Universal Religion'*. His work was essentially in the Platonic tradition, in that he was trying to express in intellectual terms, the insights gained from initiation into the sacred mysteries. His books have so far had little impact perhaps because their message belongs to the 21st century.

*The Learned Knife (1928); The Prospects of Humanism (1931); Isis and Osiris (1940); The Nameless Faith (1949); Spirit and Society (1952); I Who Am (1954); and An Introduction to Organic Philosophy: an essay on the reconciliation of the masculine and feminine principles (1955).

I will continue with extracts taken from Charlotte Waterlow's The Mystery of Karma ...... Reincarnation or Ray-incarnation?:

......From the stand-point of scientific knowledge and ordinary human experience the character of our lives often seems unintelligible. Cruel blows fall on us from unexpected quarters; patterns are woven and broken into in the most perplexing fashion; we find ourselves entangled in a web of shifting forces whose meaning is obscure. In many elements of our lives a process of organic growth or decline may be discernible, for patient work and self-discipline lay the foundations of character and achievement, while viciousness poisons our existence at its roots. But although the virtuous person to whom life has given no 'rewards' has built true from the stand-point of Eternity, the fact remains that only a certain proportion of our actions will bear fruit within the short span of an earthly existence. Our lives are conditioned from day to day by apparently erratic, random and 'unjust' forces.

A person who has spiritual faith assumes that God, Who is love, has shaped our destiny so that out of this initial condition of affliction and apparent 'injustice', we will progress after death towards a state of illumination in which the significance of all our earthly experiences will be made clear. We shall then realise that in order to unfold the attributes needed for a certain spiritual work a particular type of suffering or situation was no less essential than, say, a good education. This mystical attitude, summed up in the affirmation: 'Thy will be done', is one of the finest elements in the Christian tradition. Can we, however, fatalistically accept the view that God, in bringing us into incarnation, has plunged us into an unintelligable destiny? From the beginnings of history inspired men and women have experienced intuitions and visions about the threads of destiny which ran through their lives, and divined the existence of an underlying Pattern.

The individual on earth seems to be concerned with a very small section of an immensely complicated fabric which is being woven century by century by a vast complex of human beings. He is presented – as by a conveyer belt in a factory – with only the relatively narrow stretch of material on which he is called upon to work during his physical life. This red, gold or black thread, entwined with a multitude of others, which passes through his uncertain fingers, stretches backwards and forwards on the loom of Time, and everything depends on his power to manipulate it while it is momentarily within his grasp. To put it in more concrete terms; this foul injury, this unsolicited benediction, the inevitable and fateful entry of this woman, child, mentor, antagonist or protector into my life – these things are not matters of 'chance', but the outworking of forces set in motion long ages ago, which will be finally resolved only in ages to come. This concept not only introduces into life the fundamental elements of Destiny and Romance, but also rescues us from our bewilderment about the meaning of our earthly existence.

We can define this principle as that of 'Psychic Continuity'. A complex of relationships between individuals reappears with great exactness years or centuries later. The game is resumed at the point where it was broken off, say in the 17th. Egyptian Dynasty; each player is conditioned by advantages and disadvantages accumulated before he entered the arena, and each is called upon by Destiny to make his contribution towards straightening out the tangled skein. The elements in the equation remain the same: servant and master, wife and mistress, enemy and friend, counsellor and traitor, parent and child – and open the door to the same joy and anguish, fear and trust, satisfaction and disenchantment experienced in the past. And when the forces have thus been permitted further play, a few more steps may have been taken towards restoring the disturbed equilibrium and working out the potentialities of the original situation.

We are now brought face to face with our problem. We assume that in accordance with the principle of Psychic Continuity there are forces at work within and around us which cannot be accounted for by the influence of our present heredity and environment, and which have their origin in the remote past. But does it follow that our relationship to them must be explained in terms of Reincarnation? Most of the arguments for Reincarnation are in fact arguments for Pre-existence and Immortality. The theory of Rebirth is only a secondary hypothesis respecting the mode in which our long pilgrimage is accomplished.

Individual and Person

At this point we must clarify our terminology regarding that which incarnates.

All religions assert that there is a 'higher', deeper, more central and enduring aspect of the self than that of our everyday consciousness, which is conditioned by space and time. The terms 'ego', 'self', 'individual' and 'person' are used by most writers, Western and Eastern, in a loose fashion. But the general tradition of classical thought is clear. The individual is John or Mary in the sense that he or she exists as a differentiated entity; and such differentiation persists up to the remote point at which all distinctions ar transformed in the Absolute. We are each responsible for giving expression to our native distinctness. If we do not strive to reflect the character of the Whole precisely as it is refracted through our individual being we are guilty of insincerity. Paradoxically, the process involves the shedding of egoism and hence of separateness from others – a point which will be discussed later.

The person is something richer and more comprehensive than the mere individual. Personality implies an enlargement of individuality through sympathetic identification with others. It is the reflection in the psychological realm of the infinite potentialities of the innermost being, the soul. Individuality may be strongly marked from birth, but personality is the fruit of a long process of assimilation, co-operation and development – although it is not always easy to draw a clear line between these two aspects of the psyche.

The terms 'individual' and 'person' will be used in our discussion in this classical sense, although, as we shall see, Theosophists and some other followers of the ancient Mysteries use them in the opposite sense. They regard the individual as a <u>monad</u>, a fundamental unit of conscious life, and the personality – a word derived from the Latin <u>persona</u>, a mask – as the expression of the unregenerate, inhibited ego conditioned by heredity and environment, which the 'higher self' must redeem.

THE CLASSIC DOCTRINE OF REINCARNATION

According to H.P. Blavatsky's <u>Key to Theosophy</u>, every human being has two aspects: a permanent ego, described as the <u>individuality</u>, and its transient expression on earth, which differs in each incarnation, known as the <u>personality</u>. This ego is the soul's unchanging element in each successive incarnation and possesses a clear memory of them all. Its vehicle in each life is the personality, consisting of the lower aspect of the mind, the desire body, the physical body and its etheric double. The consciousness of the ordinary unilluminated person is centred in this complex. He lives in a world of egoism and illusion, and can act spiritually only if his higher ego manages to impress on his darkened mind the wisdom garnered in previous lives. (The terms 'individuality' and 'personality' thus have quite a different connotation from that given to them previously).

H.P.Blavatsky's successors have attempted to work out her doctrine in terms of our twentieth century knowledge of the universe. They have affirmed the existence of a nodal point, known in Hindu philosophy as <u>Antahkarana</u>, 'the point from which incarnation takes place', incarnation being a projection through the <u>Antahkarana</u> (timeless-spaceless, as far as Einsteinian conceptions are concerned) into space-time of an image of the true being or self, which transcends space and time. This image or higher ego incarnates in a whole series of personalities, each conditioned by the ones which went before. At death the higher ego withdraws into the 'astral body', the habitat of the personality. Then in due course it sheds this body, which becomes a devitalised 'shell', and finally disintegrates. At the moment of death the person is said to have a vision of all the causes which have been at work in his past life; in the case of an illuminated sage this also includes his former lives. After shedding its physical and astral vehicles, the higher ego enters a subjective state, utterly remote from all earthly conditions, known as <u>Devachan</u>, in which it dwells for a long period – usually ten to fifteen centuries – in the blissful contemplation of all that was spiritual and creative in its last incarnation. These achievements are thus gradually built into its structure, producing an increased power of control over its next expression in an earthly personality.

When the hour for rebirth strikes, the spirit awakens from this dream-like state and again enters a womb – just beforehand receiving a vision of the experiences awaiting it on earth. At this point the principle of Reincarnation becomes associated with that of <u>karma</u>. For although the former earthly personality has long ago gone out of existence, its propensities (<u>skandhas</u>) have remained latent; and they are now drawn back into manifestation by an inevitable cosmic process when the new body is formed. This occurs at the precise moment when the same combination of forces is in operation as that which determined the individual's life at the end of his previous incarnation, as are indicated in the horoscope.

The ego thus finds itself continuing an interrupted story; it meets the exact consequences of its earlier deeds. But it has no memory of those deeds because, as the former physical brain has disintegrated, its memory is stored up in the consciousness of the higher ego, which persists in the spirit state throughout the whole series of earthly lives. What has been achieved in former incarnations lives on, not in the form of memory, but of character – which is what is basically meant by karma. We are what we have made ourselves in the distant past, although the vehicles which we used in order to gain our experience have long since perished. Then at last, after a long succession of lives, we learn all the lessons which earth has to offer us, our karma becomes exhausted and we are released from the 'Wheel of Rebirth'.

This classic doctrine presents conceptual difficulties. The idea of a relatively permanent 'individuality' brooding over each successive 'personality' is not easy to grasp. The soul cannot, for instance, be said properly to 'gain experience' by its association with physical existence, for its distinctive character lies in its expression of a wisdom which is absolute and comprehensive, and which therefore anticipates and includes all possible experiences. The most that we can say is that as the process of repeated incarnations continues, the soul irradiates and transforms a series of personalities through which its distinctive nature is even more clearly expressed. For the soul always determines that which lies below itself and is never determined by it.

What is the soul's distinctive nature? It does not, surely, consist of anything derived from the succession of earthly embodiments, for it is essentially the selective principle which determines the ideal to which they are all tending. Nor does it simply embody the higher self, which is by definition universal in character. We must conclude, therefore, that we have to do with some sort of Archetype, which both partakes of the quality of the Absolute and also has a differentiated expression in time.

We must also decide in what sense 'reincarnation' has taken place. We have already seen that the so-called 'personality' is regarded as a collection of inherited tendencies, or <u>skandhas</u>. This represents one aspect of <u>karma</u>, that which determines the condition of the individual <u>internally</u>. The <u>external</u> aspect is represented by the circumstances in which he is called on to live. On the one hand he has a bad temper, on the other a privileged social position, and so on. What elements, then, in the former personality are reproduced, and by what mechanism? It is evident that, broadly speaking, physical characteristics do not reappear. If an ebony-skinned African reincarnates in a middle-class English family the child is at least outwardly indistinguishable from the other little boys at school. The ego would seem to be subject to the bodily characteristics of the race in which it is reborn. What reincarnate are 'character' and 'tendencies'. In view, however, of the modern realisation that man is a psycho-somatic organism, it is hard to see how this independence of physical heredity is achieved.

Finally, the theory of Reincarnation is naturally subject to all sorts of modifications, qualifications and refinements. It is held by some schools that rebirth is voluntary in order to gain experience, or undergone only by a minority – although how past karma is worked out if rebirth is not chosen is not made clear. Others teach that there are some cycles of history during which egos reincarnate, and some in which they do not. Again, the period between incarnations is very variously estimated. High adepts, it is alleged, are able to reincarnate imme-diately after death by an act of will. Some hold that we are reincarnated in opposite sexes alternately; some that we are born again on another planet; some that we mani-fest in turn the qualities of all the twelve zodiacal signs.

The doctrine of rebirth thus provides <u>one</u> explanation of the mysterious re-emergence of the psychic past in the present. But because certain psychic forces are re-embodied, <u>it does not follow that the personalities who originally set them in motion must be re-embodied also</u>. <u>Karma</u> could be reaped on their behalf by their spiritual descendants.

The Evidence Examined

We have suggested that the testimony of seers and philosophers and the teachings of religions are signifi-cant only if they impel us to direct investigation of the supersensible realm. When we translate the problem to the plane of the concrete we discover that it is much more complex than most investigators of the invisible world imagine. For we are in a field in which the psychology of the investigator determines the character of his discoveries.

The Soul of Nyria

The remarkable manifestation recorded by Mrs. Camp-bell Praed in her *Soul of Nyria* illustrates this complex-ity. What was the real source of the information imparted through a British medium in 1899 about the life of a little slave girl in ancient Rome? 'Miss X', the medium or instrument, was an English girl who entered into a condition of 'dissociation' under the direction of a psychologist referred to as the 'Occultist'. Mrs. Praed made a record at the sittings. The medium began to describe various features of ancient Rome. At first she spoke as any psychic might do who had been despatched on a mission by a controlling mind. But then she remarked: 'I must go back ... I shall be whipped'; and later: 'Yes, we are now in the house of Julia ... it is very fine'. She now thus spoke as a slave girl who thought herself actually back again in first century Rome. This naturally suggested that 'Miss X' was simply remembering one of her former incarnations. But then, under pressure from the 'Occultist', the psychic visited a temple which Nyria had been forbidden to enter during her life on earth. This was <u>not</u> therefore a memory of the past, but a <u>new</u> phenomenon resulting from a process initiated in London in 1899. And then, as a sequel to the record of her own existence, Nyria gave an account through another medium of the career of one of the characters in the story after she, Nyria, had died. If Nyria had been reborn as the 'Instrument' she should presumably have had no further existence outside that personality; the soul that once polarised the life energies of the Roman slave girl should have now been fully occupied in polarising those of the Victorian 'Miss X'. Yet in 1899 Nyria still thought of herself as existing on some non-physical plane of being from which the 'Occultist' and Mrs. Praed summoned her so that she could make her expeditions back into the past. Thus – Miss X: 'From what place are you speaking now?'

Nyria: 'This is not Rome. It's the sort of place I come to when you call me ... the feel of it is blue and soft and rather lonely'. This might, of course, suggest that Nyria was only a secondary personality of Miss X. But in this case the theory of Reincarnation would have to be discarded. Finally, twenty-six years later a further message from Nyria, completely consistent with the original ones, was received through an entirely different medium who knew nothing of the case! This surely suggests that the 'Instrument' was <u>not</u> simply reading her own past, that she was <u>not</u> a reincarnation of Nyria, but that she was picking up, through some chain of psychic association, either the experience of the Universal Mind, or the memory of another individual. The fact that the person who undergoes such an experience often has the impression of being the actor in the drama rather than a spectator is quite consistent with the genuineness of the operation – a point to which we will return.

Before we can be certain that a psychic impression can be attributed to reincarnation, therefore, we must first ensure that it cannot be accounted for by a wide range of other causes, such as: atavistic racial memories reflected in the 'astral light'; suggestions by a hypnotist; telepathic associations with people and places; the outworking of spiritual affinities; obsession by discarnate beings; unconscious identification with a spiritual ancestor; déjà vu; 'overshadowing' from the inner planes; spiritual infusion at birth – and perhaps false teachings inspired from the *Beyond*.

The Record of the Past

Professional psychologists tend to interpret all our transactions with the interior realms in terms of the dramatization of 'private' psychological problems. Cases of apparent or real obsession by discarnate entities, for example, are usually 'explained' by the theory of 'multiple personality'.

The theories of Jung, however, represent a half-way house, as it were, on the road towards a metaphysical evaluation of this type of figures and symbols which embody the inherited knowledge of the race. He evolved the conception of the 'collective unconscious', defined as 'that part of the individual unconscious which derives from ancestral experience'. This affirms the principle of what may be termed idealogical heredity. The responses of the race have been conditioned so powerfully and for so long in certain directions that we each have buried in our mind the accumulated memory of our ancestors and this determines our more primitive responses to life. By the mere fact of being a human I participate in a universal order of experience which I can draw upon from the deeper levels of my unconscious, levels at which it ceases to be 'my own' and becomes that of the species. This is a 'scientific' formulation of a situation which has always been familiar to inspirational thinkers. Such people are often impressed, even obsessed, by the mysterious, shadowy yet potent figures of Ancestors whose thoughts and feelings they feel to be living on in their own blood. They are obscurely aware that ancient voices are speaking to them, that the images which rise before their minds, the impulses which powerfully move them, are reinforced and confirmed by powers set in motion within human souls ages ago. The idea was expressed by Oscar Wilde: 'It is not our own soul life that we live but the lives of the dead and the soul that dwells within us is no single spiritual entity ... It is something that has dwelt in fearful places and in ancient sepulchres has made its abode'. And he added that all this was 'the result of heredity ... of concentrated race experience'.

We are thus here concerned with an alternative source of knowledge to that which is supposed to be provided by the theory of Reincarnation. The conception of our psychic inheritance form the past receives support from esoteric teachings about the 'astral plane'. Into what vehicle does the Reincarnationist conceive himself to have been born? According to what might be called orthodox unorthodox teaching, the spirit is incarnated first into the subtle ethers ; it has bodies of 'etheric' and 'astral' matter, which serve as the matrix for its spiritual envelope. The astral body is supposedly composed of a sort of psychic plasma which is impregnated with the past history of the planet. It is a miniature reflection of the 'Soul of the World', carrying within it the dark heritage of 'Adam's brood'. Manifesting as the 'Unconscious', it is charged with reflections of all the myriad thoughts and feelings which have been impressed upon the earth's psychic sphere since the beginning of time. A sensitive can therefore 'pick up' any message from the past provided that his mind is attuned to the appropriate vibration. These images and reflexes and messages may well be interpreted as reminiscences of previous incarnations. No human intermediary is necessary; it is a question of direct registration, perhaps involving the presence in the aura of nomadic planetary cell-substances, etheric particles which previously formed part of the objects which are being recalled.

Why is one picture rather than another thrown upon the censorium of the subjective mind? Jung seems to regard the emergence of such pictures as the expression of psychological conflict: the ogre which you meet in your dreams symbolizes your overdraft at the bank. But this does not explain why one particular image is selected out of thousands which would serve the same symbolical function. Nor does it explain the appearance to seers of images which clearly do <u>not</u> express inner conflict. And equally, from the 'esoteric' angle, the Past – whether we describe it as the 'storehouse of the unconscious', or as the 'Akashic records' – is accessible to us only in a very limited sense. The idea, for instance, that by a process of 'cryptaesthesia' a sensitive can raid the earlier history of the earth at will breaks down in practice. It seems that communication is effected only along certain specific channels of <u>rapport</u>; psychic omniscience is for all of such knowledge derives from some specific association with the past. It may be simply an expression of natural affinity. If in my present environment I feel particularly drawn to music, philosophy, precious stones or bee-keeping, why should I not be similarly discriminating when I attune to the past? It could be argued that such recollection derives from the <u>skandhas</u>: on reincarnation those particles which relate the individual to his previous life are drawn into a psychic nexus, and when his inner powers are stimulated the appropriate memories return. But this theory cannot be proved. Until the activity of the astral plasma within our psychic bodies is more fully understood we cannot assume that these recollections imply rebirth. They could, equally logically, derive from the inspiration of personalities on other planes who lived in previous ages, the etheric particles providing the <u>mechanism</u> of recollection. Spiritual rapport would thus be effected through chemical affinity, just as the chemistry of the genetic code provides the physical basis for psychological characteristics.

The Psychic Factor

The reincarnationist must come to terms with the phenomena of psychism.

First, experience suggests that powerful minds on earth can produce impressions telepathically on sensitive individuals which may appear to derive from influence carried over from the past. Your 'memories' of life in India may be only the thoughts of a person who lived there with whom you happen to be in telepathic rapport. And the relationship may even have a physical aspect. The child of British parents who has an Oriental cast of features has not necessarily inhabited an Oriental body in a previous incarnation; there are other ways of bringing Brighton and Benares into psychic association. According to the Mahatma Letters to the Theosophist A.P. Sinnett (p.286): 'A child may be born bearing the greatest resemblance to another person, thousands of miles away, no connection with the mother .... but whose floating image was impressed upon her soul memory, during sleep or even waking hours, and reproduced upon the sensitized plate of living flesh she carries in her'.

It is also possible that humans who have left the earth forever have cast down their likenesses upon their spiritual descendants. A person's characteristics are no more proof that he has lived before than are, say, the characteristics of a lion or a lizard. He may simply belong to a type whose members have appeared at different places throughout history.

Some people claim to have a personal recollection of a former existence on earth. Sometimes they have an uncanny knowledge of places and persons <u>still existing</u> which is attributed to memories of a very recent former incarnation, often in the same family. For example, a person may assert correctly that a door existed in an old house which has subsequently been bricked up, or may identify as his own, the toys of a child who has died. Experiences of this kind abound. A typical case was recorded in the *Occult Review* of January 1941. A boy of seven died of brain disease. For a fortnight afterwards his father, who was clairvoyant, maintained contact with him on the 'astral' plane. Then the child announced that he was 'coming home'. A little later the mother realised that she was pregnant. From that point all clairvoyant contact between father and son was broken off. Yet the boy continued to appear to him in dreams, and his aunt, who knew nothing of his announcement, reported that she herself dreamed that he was becoming younger and younger, instead of growing up, as do normal 'spirit children'. Finally his little sister dreamed that she saw him in a cot! When the baby was born he not only made astonishing progress, as if re-capitulating experience previously mastered, but seemed to be already familiar with his parents and surroundings.

Such examples appear to provide strong evidence of reincarnation. Yet they suggest only that particular individuals have been born again on earth, perhaps by displacing the soul destined for the new born baby in their eagerness to return to incarnation. They cannot <u>prove</u> that the principle applies to any greater number of persons, still less to all humanity. But if all humanity is not involved, what happens to the 'universal' law of <u>karma</u>?

An alleged memory of a previous incarnation can be explained in terms of supernormal cognition. The fact that a person finds himself familiar with the interior of a castle which he is visiting for the first time <u>may</u> point to his residence there in a former life. But it may also be the subconscious result of reading a book about the place (deja vu); of visiting it in sleep; of rapport with a deceased person who once lived in it; of telepathic contact; or of precognition. Madame Blavatsky herself realised the danger of attributing to previous incarnations experiences actually derived from psychic sensitiveness. 'The men of old, ... and medieval philosophers, ... affirmed that though this psychic phenomenon' (recognising as familiar things apparently experienced for the first time) 'was one of the greatest arguments in favour of immortality and the soul's pre-existence, the latter being endowed with an individual memory apart from the physical brain, it is no proof of reincarnation. Dreams, forebodings, prescience ... are impressions left by our astral spirit on our brain, which receives them more or less distinctly, according to the proportion of blood with which it is supplied during the hours of sleep'. (*Isis Unveiled Vol.1, p.179*). On the plane of sub-conscious thought, mind communes with mind. People are responding today to all sorts of ideas and fantasies which are being broadcast, as it were, by multitudes of other personalities, incarnate and discarnate. Their thoughts are often merely psychic reflexes. They are 'tuning in' all over the place, picking up indiscriminately whatever happens to be floating around in their 'astral' surroundings – memories, pictures, manifestations of elemental life, or even images deliberately presented to them by powerful minds in this world or the next. At the lowest level the sensitive becomes the wretched instrument of sinister intelligences, a powerless automaton who objectifies evil influences initiated outside himself. This we call 'obsession'. Ordinary people who have not sunk to this state are nevertheless far less their own masters than they suppose. Only the truly spiritual person is able freely to express his own inner life, deliberately appropriating from the great sphere of psychic being around him that which he deems of value. It is significant that in the Rosicrucian Order the highest degree is that attained by the individual who has become *ipsissimus* – 'his very self'.

The extreme case of subjection to the influence of another mind is that of 'possession'. There is abundant evidence that control of the body of a sensitive can be completely taken over by another personality. In the case of the 'Watseka Wonder' a girl woke up one morning manifesting all the psychological and mental characteristics of another girl, unknown to her, who had died some years before, including full knowledge of all the circumstances of the dead girl's life. The identification was so complete that she was adopted by the dead girls's parents. But lo! one day her normal self reappeared and retained control of its original earthly vehicle throughout the rest of her life. If a person is capable of acting, thinking and feeling as another for long periods by a process of psychic attunement, we must be cautious in attributing to rebirth what may only be an extreme case of rapport.

The fact that the normal owner of a body can be ejected from it when he or she has grown up naturally in it suggests that such a displacement could occur at the very hour of birth, preventing the ordained occupant from manifesting at all! In such cases the controlling entity may withdraw at some point in the person's life, thus indicating that rebirth has not taken place. It is notable that a large number of the recorded cases from the Orient, whose inhabitants are generally more receptive to psychic impressions than the 'tough-minded' Westerners.

The Testimony of Spiritualism

Let us consider the evidence provided by spiritualistic communications. (The correct term should be 'spiritism'. 'Spiritualism' properly describes the philosophic doctrine that reality consists of units of consciousness, or spiritual monads; and it is used in this sense in the Continent of Europe but the use of the word 'spiritualism' to describe 'spiritism' has become firmly established in England and America). Experience shows that recently departed spirits, normally manifesting through mediums, embrace a wide variety of doctrines about rebirth.

The Spirits' views are evidently determined by two basic factors. First, they appear to continue to hold for a long period the same ideas about spiritual things which they embraced on earth. Second, when they have become discarnate they are apparently just as liable to be inculcated with new, and perhaps misleading, doctrines as they were in the body. The conditions in the 'spirit spheres' appear to be much the same as on earth: all possible opinions, enlightened and unenlightened, have their eager representatives and we must rely on our native discrimination to sort them out.

Spiritualism and Occult Science

We can, however, set our feet on far firmer ground than that of the inconclusive evidence presented through mediumistic channels by examining the principles of occults science, handed down to genuine seekers for thousands of years.

The attitude adopted by students of esotericism to this problem varies. All tend to regard spiritualism with suspicion. Some assert that nothing more is involved than 'bhuta-worship' – dealings with vitalize astral 'shells' which deceptively simulate the lives of those who have cast them off in their progress to higher states of being. These ideas became influential through H.P. Blavatsky but certain facts speak for themselves.

First, history suggests that for thousands of years humanity in general was cut off from the higher spheres. Only a tiny minority of seers, sages and mystics emerged into the sunlight of true spiritual glory. The majority believed in communing with spirits, but could contact only those who were on a low level of consciousness. This would justify the view of most occultists that intercourse with the dead is an uncertain and unjustifiable business. But in the modern age something unprecedented in the history of the planet seems to be taking place as we have suggested previously. Doors previously closed are being thrown open so that power and illumination of a new order is pouring forth from the heavenly realms to many in physical embodiment. The first phases of modern spiritualism were relatively crude, but a movement has started which has untold possibilities. If by a right adjustment of the mind you can place yourself in touch with your deceased relatives and friends, there is in principle no reason why you should not carry the process further and communicate, first with 'guides' and teachers and ultimately with very exalted souls.

Association with the inner planes is naturally fraught with the dangers of illusion and deception. Nevertheless, any sane person can distinguish between a living presence and a dead echo of the past. It is in fact just the sense of being in contact with a human personality who is unmistakably alive, intelligent and capable of creative action which impresses the witnesses of a powerful display of mediumship. The manifesting personality may perhaps be commonplace, but he or she is there before one, speaking, thinking and dealing with new situations as we do ourselves – this is what it is impossible to forget, or explain away.

What, then, do the spirits say about Reincarnation? In the great realm of the Unseen to which souls proceed after death there is an infinity of regions, each with its characteristic philosophy and customs. ('In my Father's House are many mansions'). The spirits who inhabit many of these regions often teach the doctrine of Reincarnation. Is this because they are fully emancipated or is it because they know nothing beyond the beliefs which prevail in their particular realm? The dwellers in a certain spirit realm who are ignorant of any more exalted state of being than their own and who believe in reincarnation will naturally conclude that the souls who depart from their midst to higher planes have descended again to earth to be reborn.

The confirmation of theories of Reincarnation by testimony from beyond the Veil is therefore of uncertain value. The believer in Reincarnation will be drawn after death to a place where he finds congenial spirits who firmly embrace the doctrine, and he will perhaps seek to communicate the good news through some channel to his associates on earth, and he who holds the opposite view will do the same.

But it is possible to advance beyond this point. Much testimony indicates that experience out of the physical body is determined by the principle of rapport. Consequently that which is beyond the range of an individual's power of response does not yet exist for him. A spirit inhabiting a more inferior dimension of being may be in his proximity but he will not perceive him or her until his mind is adjusted to a finer order of vibration, nor will he know anything of the more emancipated realm from which that spirit comes. It is as if here on earth a man could not see a concert hall until he had become awakened to the possibilities of music, or a church until religious feeling had been stirred within him. The key to the evaluation of the testimony of spiritualism about Rebirth is to discover what is taught on the subject by exalted souls. But how does one get in touch with them? In accordance with the basic law of rapport, holy and wise spirits are drawn to mortals who are wise and holy. If, therefore, we want light on these deep problems from spirits, we must start by transforming our own natures.

Having considered the evidence for Reincarnation, I turn now to the difficulties which the concept presents.

Normal and Abnormal

First, let us note the explanation which the doctrine of Reincarnation offers for the wide diversity of human conditions. The varieties of situation and fate of individuals are so extraordinary and often so apparently unrelated to their character and behaviour that the theory of Rebirth may well seem to be the only philosophy which makes sense of it all. The extreme inequalities and injustices which prevail can be explained in terms of the doctrine of <u>karma</u> as the outworking of forces set in motion by people who lived in the past. But what is the normal character of human relationships when they are <u>not</u> distorted by <u>karmic</u> influences? If the great Plan for humanity requires individuals to develop every possible type of talent and capacity for the glory of God, then their respective situations are bound to involve a measure of apparent 'inequality'. For apart from <u>karmic</u> complications, there are all sorts of factors, such as poverty, isolation, inferior social status, physical hardship and even sickness, which are essential for the unfoldment of different types of consciousness. Is a sea captain involved with 'bad <u>karma</u>' because he has to struggle with storms, mutinies and wrecks? Are a strong character's early struggles, which he later looks back on with gratitude, the expression of an evil influence? Is it 'misfortune' to become an orator through overcoming a stammer? And conversely, does not a great deal of what reincarnationists regard as 'good <u>karma</u>' appear unfortunate from a spiritual stand-point? Man is surely like a tree whose growth is fostered by every type of experience, both tough and tender. We do not exercise our fingers by playing only the white keys of the piano. We should be wary of attributing to 'bad <u>karma</u>' experiences which may be the essential conditions of spiritual unfoldment. Only when a person has attained an adequate conception of the Divine Order as it is expressed on earth can he gain a clear picture of the irregularities which result from departing from it. Incarnation means nothing unless the cup is drained to the full.

The Nature of Genius

The principle of Rebirth has often been invoked to explain the phenomenon of 'genius'. How else can one account for the precocity of a Mozart or a Clerk Mazwell? (The converse situation entailed in the painful degeneration of the powers of Cicero or Leonardo da Vinci in their modern reincarnation in this or that celebrity raises a problem which the Reincarnationists have not apparently faced!).

The Reincarnationists' explanation of genius assumes that spiritual powers are attained only by a process of education in earlier lives. Little Rudolf's struggles with the piano are thus the beginning of a development which will culminate in ages to come in his birth as a musical genius. And conversely, Shakespeare, Newton and other geniuses secured their triumph by carrying further the amateurish achievements of earlier incarnations.

Can this explanation satisfy us? Another explanation lies in the possibility that the genius is inspired by a discarnate personality. This is suggested by the case of 'prodigies' whose powers suddenly leave them at some point in their lives. Such a degeneration might, of course, be caused by some process at work within the individual's own organism. But it could also be caused by the withdrawal of the discarnate being.

This brings us back to the conception of 'overshadowing'. Lofty attainment on the earth plane may express the inspiration of lofty souls in the Invisible. If I am filled with love, wisdom, the power to lead people, it is because I am in soul unity with discarnate personalities who manifest these qualities in greater perfection. If I develop remarkable talents as a teacher, explorer, scientist or artist, it is because those who possess these talents in higher measure are inspiring me from the Unseen.

A deep philosophical issue is involved. It seems to be open to God, if He so wills, to create persons whose faculties express an unimpeded flow of divine power into the soul. Such geniuses as Leibnitz, Bach and Velasquez may not after all have created their works by the ingenious feat of standing repeatedly on their own shoulders, but simply because God fashioned them in that way! 'Genius' may thus be simply the effect produced when the revelation of the divine nature in man is not distorted by the working out of 'bad karma'. The same principle applies to saintliness, heroism and other sublime manifestations of the human personality. A long process of preparation may well underlie lives of creative service. But it does not follow that the stages in that preparation have all been accomplished by the same person through a series of earthly embodiments. It may be a question, rather, of preparing the soil through a chain of different individuals for the appearance of a supreme manifestation of a particular Life Ray.

Rebirth, Continuity and Variety

There are further problems regarding the working of the law of karma. Its action must make for continuity between the present and the past. Yet it is difficult to see how the activity of the skandhas, which come into manifestation again after the inter-incarnation period, can account for the appearance of an individual whose situation and capacities are very different from those of the one who originally passed them on. If a person has spent most of his earthly existence in dubious financial machinations, the impulses which he generated should produce the same tendencies after his rebirth. But they could hardly find expression in, say, the life of a violinist or a social worker. Unless the past is carried over fully into the present the principle of <u>karma</u> loses its significance. Yet this principle would seem to be inconsistent with another re-incarnationist theory: that we progress through a series of widely diversified embodiments in order to expand our experience. For the more differentiated each incarnation is, the more difficult does it become to explain it as the outworking of those which have preceded it. Theosophical literature asserts that: 'The Self or Monad is the same, but the aspect of it manifesting at each point may be quite different, and even unrecognisable. By reincarnating, eventually, 'all round the clock', however, the Self acquires a personality field of catholic powers, and becomes a whole and perfect man, by the limitations of ordinary humanity are transcended'. Or again: 'A Napoleon or a Caesar in one life may be a good and tender mother in another, and a poet or musician in a third'.

This conception is fundamentally unsatisfactory. It is easy to conjure up a romantic picture of the same soul incarnating successively as a dwarf, a philosopher, a prostitute, a sea captain, a dog fancier, a mathematician and a mother of ten, but the more we try to understand how such an elaborate process of transmogrification can be achieved, the more bewildered we become. For apart from morbid cases of psychological dissociation and multiple personality, we know nothing of departmentalised egos. On the contrary, every man and woman we meet is first and foremost a distinct <u>person,</u> however manifold and intricate his characteristics. The more mature and individual, the more definite and distinct his personality. The reincarnationists make some attempt to provide for this factor by asserting that our earthly personality is a limited projection into space and time of a transcendental self endowed with limitless potentialities. One bit of it can appear on the scene as a queen or an admiral and another as the young lady at the cash desk, the Sage of Concord (the American philosopher Emerson), convict No: 185769, or you or me. A dip in the metaphysical lucky bag may bring up almost anything we can conceive! But here again, if the net is too widely thrown, the image of the basic self behind all these diverse manifestations ceases to have any significance as a unifying principle, and merges into that of a collection or syndicate of spirits. The conception of the individual as in any serious sense a <u>person</u> is completely lost.

The idea behind these assertions is, however, of major importance. Our personalities <u>are</u> limited, pathetic and conditioned manifestations of something far more comprehensive and fundamental. We can at the most strike but one note in a complete chord. The conception is intrinsically sound; but in formulating it in terms of the evolution of a <u>monad</u> the Theosophists have seriously confused the issues. For in attempting to invest it with a universal character they have given it characteristics which cannot accord with its distinctive nature. Leibnitz, who introduced the concept of the monad into Western philosophy, made no such error. In his system each unit of consciousness is a comprehensive whole, and the 'universal harmony' is achieved, not by endowing every monad with contradictory qualities, but by the unity which exists basically between them all.

The reincarnationists would seem therefore to have confused the progressive universalisation of the individual with his progressive union with other individuals. The difference is fundamental. If we regard each unit of human consciousness as an unique expression of the character of a type, the quality of a spiritual ray, then the possibilities are limitless. It is open to each soul to strike his divine note with ever greater fulness, throughout Eternity. Even when he becomes veritably a god, he will still be manifesting a distinctive aspect of cosmic reality. However rich his experience, there will always be a dominant key, a differentiated function in terms of which he is called upon to radiate forth the Divine Life. The reincarnationists seek to secure this comprehensive manifestation by making the fantastic postulate that the individual becomes, for the duration of an incarnation, something fundamentally incompatible with his own self. The doctrine of the Life Ray asserts that it is achieved through union with the members of one's own spiritual family. This implies both the preservation of distinctness – without which all becomes chaos – and the closest possible participation in the lives of one's associates through love. Their characters are known and their experiences are shared through spiritual empathy, so that perfect co-operation becomes possible. Here on earth we often have a preliminary experience of this unity. We find that when we truly love another person, our respective personalities are both enhanced and blended. In his strange poem *The Phoenix and the Turtle* Shakespeare makes the point:

> *So they loved, as love in twain*
> *Had the essence but in one:*
> *Two distincts, division none:*
> *Number there in love was slain...*

Reason, in itself confided,
Saw division grow together:
To themselves yet either-neither,

Simple was so well compounded
That it cried: How true a twain
Seemeth this concordant one!
Love hath reason, reason none
If what parts can so remain.

And this principle is in accord with the divine order which we shall one day know in fullness when we have entered the realms of Light and taken our place in that Celestial Company to which we truly belong.

The notion that anybody may appear anywhere as anybody in defiance of all principles of organic order represents in an acute form the problem of reconciling a string of diversified lives with the unswerving operation of the law of <u>karma</u>. For if the purpose of a given incarnation is to work out the consequences of a previous one, how are we to relate this to the doctrine that only one aspect of the Self is manifested on earth in any one life? If we assume, for example, that life number seven is not an outworking of lives numbers one to six, but a brand new expression of the transcendental ego, then it will either initiate, or be a link in, a different chain of causation. Alternatively, if it is actually determined by forces set in motion in lives one to six, then it is unclear why the projection of one part of the Self should have to deal with the outcome of the behaviour of another with widely different characteristics! The Theosophists assert that since the progress of history is accomplished in terms of cycles (an Oriental hypothesis which many Western historians would not accept), we are concerned with a spiral structure. A particular incarnation may have no evident relationship to those which precede and follow it, but it will be in character with one which corresponds to it at an equivalent point of another turn of the spiral. Thus your karma from, say, a life in ancient Rome will find expression only when you are born in a period of history which is a cyclic repetition of Roman history. All such notions are, however, highly speculative, and are vitiated, as we have seen, by a fundamentally unsatisfactory conception of the monad.

We Have Met Before

The same problem regarding the claims of the original and the reinforced occurs in the sphere of human relationships. A sense of deep mutual recognition between sensitive individuals does not prove that history is psychically repeating itself. Certain persons may naturally be in harmonious relationship, so that they feel a spontaneous familiarity and joy when they meet. It is as if they belonged to the same spiritual family. Equally, if two people find each other repellent, it does not follow that they are resuming an ancient feud; it may simply be that their natures are so different that association is naturally difficult. Neither the rapture awakened in our souls by the personalities whom we adore nor the revulsion produced by those whom we detest necessarily involves encounters in previous lives.

Reincarnation cuts us off from our Affinities

A major danger presented by the theory of Rebirth is that it distorts our whole picture of the size and activities of the planet's invisible population. For the Reincarnation hypothesis would seem to be based on the assumption that the number of souls in the world is roughly constant, and that this number continually reappears on the earth in an endless variety of situations and relationships until the great drama has been fully worked out. (The doctrine was, of course, developed before the 20th century population explosion occurred). But if what are believed to be the previous incarnations of a single individual are really the incarnations of a series of <u>different</u> human beings, who after death have continued their evolution on other planes of life, then there must be an immeasurably greater number of personalities active within the psychic sphere of the earth than is conceived of by the reincarnationists. It is a simple matter of arithmetic. The reincarnationists are virtually dividing the total population of the planet by the number of alleged reincarnations which have taken place in the course of its history – an enormous reduction in the number of its inhabitants! Substitute for a supposed long chain of past lives a chain of personalities who <u>continue to exist</u> in other spheres of being, and you have a very different picture of the situation. The principle of unique incarnation implies that an enormous number of souls will be incarnated in the course of the planet's life history. But the Creator works on a scale which is beyond the grasp of the human mind. And in the more interior realms of being separate individuals, as we know them here, may blend into units of consciousness of a higher order – a mystical teaching which we shall consider later.

On the basis of the orthodox theory, when those who were once born on earth are not reincarnated, they are likely to be in a condition in which it is undesirable or impossible to communicate with them. They may be earth-bound spirits, with whom association is unprofitable. Or they may have risen into the subjective <u>Devachanic</u> state, where they are remote from our human concerns, so that we can commune with them only by projecting ourselves into <u>their</u> world.

Everything therefore turns upon whether there really are non-physical, objective realms of spiritual being whose inhabitants can cast down their energy and illumination to our suffering earth. According to most Oriental Schools, such realms do <u>not</u> exist. There is the physical plane; there is a distant realm, about which we know almost nothing, in which the emancipated souls dwell; and for the mass of deceased humanity there is a dream world of purely subjective experience. 'You said that we sometimes meet our friends beyond the veil of death – when?' enquired a questioner wistfully of a Buddhist Master. His answer was: 'On our return to earth. The intervening worlds are entirely subjective.' Many Occidental philosophers take the same view. For such a Platonist as Dr. Inge, for instance, all after-death states short of absorption in the Eternal have a dreamy and deceptive character; and in his *Perennial Philosophy* Aldous Huxley indicated that he also was very doubtful about the reality of the different 'heavens' which people supposedly enter after death. To Western reincarnationists the conception of <u>Devachan</u> is fundamental. Thus they fail to allow for the existence of hosts of evolved beings who are <u>active</u> in the psychic sphere of the planet. According to the theory, such beings <u>simply cannot be there</u>. But what if they <u>are</u> there! If so, the reincarnationists are failing to take account of a vast range of unseen activity which conditions our lives all the time.

They may assert, for example, that a person who was born in ancient Thebes has reincarnated in modern London. But such an assertion will ignore some four thousand years of post-mortem unfoldment and achievement in non-physical spheres. It is an occult principle that there is no realisation without <u>rapport</u>. The reincarnationists therefore cut themselves off from the inspiration and power of the great company of the Risen. They misinterpret the wonderful ministry continuously poured out from higher planes as good <u>karma</u> inherited from previous incarnations. The present is certainly determined by the past. but 'good <u>karma</u>' simply means that the individual soul is capable of responding to the beneficent forces at work in the universe, which operate, not only through earth-dwellers but through invisible beings with whom that soul is linked by arcane bonds. It is a matter not of the mechanical outworking of a dead past, but of a continuous communion between the living and the Risen.

PROGRESS AND EMBODIMENT

We must now consider the deeper moral implications of the theory of Reincarnation. Does the scheme of Rebirth really suggest a wise ordaining of human destiny?

The idea that a person deepens and extends his knowledge through a series of lives filled with experimentation, adventure, education and suffering implies that a large part of each incarnation will be devoted to repeating the <u>least</u> significant elements in his previous experience. The whole wearisome business the cot, the kindergarten, the adolescent love affair, apprenticeship and 'growing up' generally must be gone through again and again in order to place the individual in a situation in which he can learn the <u>really</u> important lessons of life. On this theory true experience, in the sense that life's earlier lessons are carried a stage further, is only possible when the organism has been repeatedly adapted to respond to it. It cannot, of course, be <u>proved</u> that such a toilsome system is not really operative. But our intuitions suggest that the principle of Divine Economy provides a less oppressive pathway for human progress.

From our earliest years many of us have a feeling that, however many regressions and set-backs may occur, we are essentially growing psychologically. Unless we have inwardly fossilised, our mental horizon gradually extends, our latent powers gradually unfold, and we are conscious that, through suffering, danger and disappointment, our true selves are coming into expression. Any reversal of this process is regarded as unhealthy. Infantilism or fixation in an adult repels us – just because we are so deeply aware that the individual's true path is onward and upward. But most of us, when the time comes to 'die', are dwelling in the framework of a mental and moral edifice which we have only just begun to build. We have on our hands a mass of unresolved problems, unrealised projects, unrequited feelings, and undeveloped capacities. We realise that it would take the equivalent of a whole series of earthly lives to work out the forces which have been set in motion in the course of a few brief years. Yet it is suggested that this process of expression and fulfilment should take the form of a weary succession of 'black-outs', the soul being repeatedly pushed back into a condition of infantile impotence and ignorance!

There is also the question of Divine Mercy. Physical existence is in many ways a grievous burden upon the spirit. It is a momentous and critical episode in the history of the soul, whose true significance will only be revealed to us when we have attained spiritual illumination. We must hesitate to conclude, therefore, that the path which the Creator has ordained for mankind involves repeated spells of such a condition.

Finally, the ancient conception of periodical withdrawals into the state of <u>Devachan</u> may be a misconception of the real truth about the post-mortem condition of the soul. At a certain point in its evolution after death the soul may well need to retire into a deep subjective state to contemplate the higher elements in its experience. But this does not mean that such withdrawals must necessarily be the basic condition of its attainment of emancipation. For this implies a sort of spiritual schizophrenia – periods of objective awareness on earth, with a tenuous relation to the interior realms of being, alternating with periods of subjective awareness in a fairyland paradise free from all disturbing memories of earth. The ego is then never in touch with Reality at all, for while in the body it is living in a waking dream, and while in Devachan it is living in a realm of elevated fantasy.

The philosophy of Spiritualism surely provides a more reasonable account of man's situation. It asserts that the reward for aspiration and striving on earth is a progressive awakening on planes of spiritual existence which are more <u>real</u> either than the space-time realm of bodily existence or the dream-Nirvana of Devachan. The result of behaving with integrity and righteousness on earth is the emancipation of the ego, stage by stage, from different orders of illusion. Make yourself real during your physical life, and after death you will drawn irresistibly into a realm of real being. You will 'go to your own place'. Is not this one of the applications of the Law of <u>Karma</u>?

The Lessons of Earth

According to the theory of Reincarnation, a great deal of the experience acquired in each earth life is mere recapitulation; and even that which we <u>do</u> appropriate when we have built up the physical organism does not refer <u>primarily</u> to the physical plane of existence. We have very few experiences which are exclusively <u>of</u> the earth – even though they may be accumulated <u>on</u> the earth. Perhaps the best way of identifying them is by considering the type of sensations which, according to the spiritualists, earth-bound spirits seek to obtain by obsessing mortals. They seem to be avid for experiences which they can no longer enjoy in their discarnate state: Contact with matter as a solid medium which both opposes and supports the soul, physical sex, stimuli derived from food, drink and drugs and so on. But all that we learn from transcendental sources regarding the state of the soul after death, or when active in trance or sleep, suggests that the organs of perception of the 'subtle body' open the door to far more wonderful possibilities than the experiences of the physical organs. And even when we are in the body our mode of cognition is <u>primarily</u> psychic; we register via the physical brain what can in fact be registered directly and with far greater sensitivity by the mind through the less resistant medium of 'etheric' matter. In any case, the deeper experiences of life are only <u>incidentally</u> acquired through the physical body. There are evidently great ranges of experiences which do not require physical incarnation. Thus the process of thought consists in establishing relations between phenomena as such; it is of no significance whether they are physical or etheric. This applies to the contemplation of beauty; to union with other beings in love; to the exercise of the will; to the experience of such essentially spiritual emotions as joy or remorse. All the activities which relate to the higher life of the soul, such as aspiration, self-discipline, purification and worship, have no necessary connection with physical matter.

Incarnation is an essential experience for the soul, for at some point it must touch that outward periphery of experience at which the great involutionary journey ends and the return path begins. But it is not easy to determine how prolonged an association with matter is necessary to provide a unit of consciousness with the minimum essential experiences of embodiment; a whole series of lives in different bodies; or one breath; or even seclusion in a womb? It may be that all that essentially matters is that the soul should <u>touch</u> earth. A long life in a physical body can produce a rich harvest. But it may suffice if what is in essence an emanation from the unconditioned realm of Spirit knows for an instant the limitation of physical incarnation.

We have already referred to the ancient doctrine of Involution and Evolution. According to this teaching the soul descends from an interior sphere of being in a <u>subjective</u> state. In its descent it passes through, and relates itself to, plane after plane of non-physical being, whose conditions became gradually denser and of a semi-material nature as it draws near to the physical realm. At birth a major transition occurs: it awakens into objective consciousness, and from that moment begins the long journey back to its Origin. In the first phase of this pilgrimage home it is in a condition of little more than incubation; for however alive and alert we may feel on earth, we are still really living only in a womb. We are imprisoned briefly in a three-dimensional world, in order that our souls may be subjected to a process of individualisation. Then, at physical death, we experience our second birth into the states in which our full development will take place. As we progress through these states we enter successively in objective consciousness those realms of being which we had passed through subjectively on our journey towards earth; and we may have faint recollections of their character – which the human mind may interpret as recollections of previous embodiments.

If physical incarnation is the turning point between the process of the soul's descent into objective self-expression and the process of its evolutionary return to its Home, then it may not be to our advantage either to prolong it beyond its natural span or to repeat it. Any lingering at the decisive hairpin bend in this immense pilgrimage would be equivalent to mistaking the halfway house for the terminus! The situation may indeed be out of our control. For if the mighty impulse towards incarnation is reversed when the culminating point of physical incarnation is reached, it will then irresistibly swing the individual back along the return path towards the inner realms of being, whether he wills it or not.

Here we must note two further teachings. First, it is an occult law that it is always possible to re-enter any condition with which one has once made contact. If the vibration of the physical realm has been duly registered, the soul can respond to that realm again thousands of years later, even though it exists now in utterly different conditions. Thus it is possible for the disembodied, as they labour for the salvation of humanity, to project into the physical realm the high vibrations which heal and redeem. The ladder can be ascended and descended at will. Secondly, it does not follow that a person who dies in infancy is deprived of essential earth experience; he may be able to acquire this experience by subjective association with the living. Psychically sensitive children, for instance, are sometimes conscious of 'invisible play-mates', who may be gaining by attunement the experience which the Reincarnationists assert can only be learned by submitting to rebirth.

The Doctrine of Ascension

The idea of rebirth conflicts with our actual experience of spiritual growth. If we live rightly we come to realise that as the body weakens, the soul is slowly maturing. Year by year we become more aware of the manifold threads which we will one day weave into a shining pattern. If we are spiritually alive, death will appear to us as a doorway to a wider life in which we will realise our frustrated hopes and unfold our latent potentialities. At the end of our period of physical incarnation, therefore, we shall not be a worn-out machine, but an organism ripe for further growth. In our earthly years of toil, suffering, adventure and discipline we will have laid a foundation on which we can build for ages to come. Our intuitions tell us that the outworkings in other spheres of being of the experiences of even a most restricted period of physical existence can be indescribably wonderful. An obscure recognition of this fact often impels us to treat the smallest episodes with deep responsibility; we realise subconsciously that we are concerned with germinal elements of life out of which wider situations will unfold after death.We die on the threshold of life. Our physical existence is a period of seed-growth; its flowers and fruits appear in other realms of being. Man must be thought of as rising forever <u>upward</u>, through sphere after sphere, continually growing in knowledge and experience towards the status of godhead, and from time to time turning back to earth, not to learn again what has already been sufficiently absorbed, but to lift others up to the level of consciousness which he has now reached. The possibilities which life on earth offers us for acquiring deep spiritual knowledge are relatively small. We should, of course, seek to live in Eternity here and now, and there are exceptional personalities who succeed in doing this. But they are subjected to a great strain, for present conditions make it hard for them to break through to the Source of their inspiration and power. Often they can experience only fragmentary insights into the condition which awaits them after death. Their labour consists far more in maintaining an outpost in the realms of <u>maya</u> than in unfolding the potentialities of their souls in full measure.

When an individual dedicates himself to the spiritual life he begins to withdraw inwardly from <u>attachment</u> to earthly conditions, and to associate himself as fully as possible with the <u>next</u> world in order to equip himself to serve in <u>this</u> world in what the great Hindu scripture, the <u>Bhagavadgita</u>, calls 'consecrated action'. A series of physical incarnations does <u>not</u> offer a path to transcendental realisation. It <u>does</u> offer a unique opportunity for individualisation; but tremendous possibilities for 'character building' may equally be available on other planes of being. Since for most people life on earth is a school of fortitude rather than of illumination, repeated incarnations would provide the soul with only a fragment of the enlightenment which it could gain by rising upwards towards the Light.

The only logical interpretation of the doctrine of Reincarnation is to regard it as an involuntary process by which man is drawn into the physical realm by an irresistible force in order to reap the karma of his previous deeds on earth. Yet this enterprise could be self-defeating, for in returning repeatedly into conditions of darkness and exile the individual might continually generate evil karma, thus delaying his liberation indefinitely. This grim prospect should impel us to consider the alternative doctrine that after death people redeem their evil deeds through 'overshadowing' their spiritual descendants, and that when this labour is completed the whole spiritual group ascends into realms of fulfilment and release. The reincarnationist does not realise that the truth and freedom which he regards as the reward for patient experimentation on the earthly level are accessible to him here and now if he follows the mystical path. He imposes upon himself the task of crawling for millenia round the rim of the Wheel instead of moving inwards along one of its spokes towards the Hub. He thus becomes polarised towards earth, and insensitive to that great realm inhabited by exalted beings who are ever seeking to draw humanity up to their level, and so he remains out of rapport with the deeper sources of regeneration. When he dies, therefore, he enters the next world facing in the wrong direction – back towards instead of away from the physical body. Although the reincarnationist has appreciated that the growth towards Release must normally take a long time, he makes the mistake of picturing this progress as accomplished in a <u>lateral</u> direction, through a long series of earthly lives. Philosophical spiritualism asserts that the journey is essentially upward, through planes of objective non-physical being, which provide the conditions necessary for unfoldment. This is surely the significance of the scriptural saying: 'Now is the time for salvation'. There is a direct path upward on which we can set our feet at once; and leads away from earth. To assert that nothing more awaits us after death than entry into a temporary subjective state, followed by a return into conditions of extreme limitation, is to condemn us to weariness, oppression and sorrow for ages to come.

Reincarnation and Morality

We must now consider the moral implications of the theory of Reincarnation. The fundamental elements in the spiritual life – belief in the Ultimate Reality; confidence that through attunement with this Reality, man can escape from spiritual darkness and illusion; recognition that every person is a child of God, and that love is the key to creation – are affirmed by religious people whether or not they are reincarnationists. The doctrine of Rebirth relates only to the <u>mechanism</u> by which man accomplishes his long journey towards final emancipation. The history of many of the saints shows that the highest order of spirituality can be attained without giving any thought to such metaphysical problems. Moreover, from one point of view the doctrine of Rebirth is materialistic, and <u>any</u> form of materialism exacts a certain price.

First, the reincarnationists tend to assume that wisdom is the product of an extended process of trial and error. They suggest, for instance, that 'the voice of conscience is only the summarised memory of past experiences, the instinctive remembrance of the errors which have been committed in past lives and the sufferings which have ensued'. This suggests that the basis of our higher knowledge is merely empirical, and thereby reduces intuitions to the level of summations of past experience which never acquire any absolute value. This is a surprising assertion from those who take their stand on a transcendental philosophy, which postulates that the soul perceives truth by direct illumination by The Light of Heaven! The truth, we suggest, is that the vicissitudes of life gradually make the individual receptive to the inspiration of his soul – by no means the same thing as the reincarnationist – and Freudian – idea that 'conscience' is the fruit of experience. And this inspiration moves him to ascend vertically, as it were, into the spheres of Light, from which further bondage to the body would cut him off.

There is also the question of the psychology of the soi-disant re-embodied. It is romantic to believe oneself involved in a complicated and exciting plot which unravels with the slow progress of history, a drama in which one has already played a series of parts. But the extent to which the disciples of Jesus, and the saints, poets, artists, philosophers, kings, statesmen and courtesans of history have supposedly reincarnated today in apparently ordinary people is disconcerting! The idea that the torch of Socrates, Dante or Erasmus has been passed on by the mechanism of karma into their somewhat unsteady hands savours of spiritual vulgarity!

When we turn from the past to the future we are met with further problems. The doctrine opens the door to procrastination. The consoling thought that there are other lives ahead of us in which we can make up for our present shortcomings tempts us to put off the evil day when we must at last come to terms with reality. Evidence of this attitude is provided by the inertia and sterility which have paralysed the creative forces in many Oriental countries; the general belief in Reincarnation has made progress seem an infinitely receding factor in the equation – something to be achieved 'next time'. From this point of view the secularity and agnosticism inculcated in these countries by Western modernisation may be a healthy development.

The doctrine also encourages calculating self-interest; the temptation to lay up for oneself a psychic nest-egg of 'good <u>karma</u>' from which one hopes to profit in lives to come. The fact that life-to-life progress is regarded as an individualistic affair (I shall gain or suffer this or that) tends to foster an attitude of spiritual acquisitiveness. There is nothing inherent in the principle of <u>karma</u> to move man to apply it on the spiritual level. What is needed is a teaching which places the <u>karmic</u> situation safely above the plane of individualism, involving the mystical redemption of the deeds of others.

<u>The Doctrine of Reincarnation cannot Teach us about Love</u>

It is possible that the Reincarnationists have exaggerated the importance of the great principle of action and reaction. According to their theory the 'lessons' of previous lives are gathered up and assimilated only in that inter-incarnation state in which the individual reviews his past history from a remote transcendental vantage-point – a conception which we have already seen presents serious difficulties. During his waking life the reincarnationist is in exactly the same position as all the rest of us. Fate deals him all sorts of unexpected and apparently 'unjust' blows, or bestows equally perplexing gifts. And he concludes that all this welter of unintelligible happenings <u>must</u> represent the outworking of forces which he himself set in motion during earlier incarnations. When after death he is drawn back into the Within he will, he believes, be able to piece the pattern together and see just why his life took that particular course. But until that hour strikes he <u>knows</u> nothing about the deeper origins of his present situation. The original causes of his unhappy marriage, his financial failure, his wretched health, his uncanny luck or his linguistic ability are veiled from his eyes, embodied in the inaccessible history of his reputed former existences in Iberia or Tibet. Philosophical reflections about the operation of the Law of <u>Karma</u> are therefore unlikely to aid us much in the real problems of life. The true keys to fortitude and illumination are provided by a mystical order of revelation in the light of which such considerations are irrelevant. The spiritual seeker is finally content to accept God's inscrutable Will in faith; and when his grumblings and his speculations cease, illumination comes. Job's complaints died on his lips when God revealed Himself to him: 'I have heard of thee by the hearing of the ear, but now mine eye seeth thee. Wherefore I abhor myself, and repent in dust and ashes'. The God Krishna, after allowing the hero of the Bhagavadgita, Arjuna, to argue with him for some time about his <u>karma</u>, finally revealed Himself in His full Godhead. 'Thou hast now seen face to face my form divine so hard to see; for even the gods in heaven ever long to see what thou hast seen. Not by the Vedas, or an austere life, or gifts to the poor, or ritual offerings can I be seen as thou hast seen me. Only by love can men see me, and know me, and come unto me. He who works for me, who loves me, whose End Supreme I am, free from attachment to all things, and with love for all creation, he in truth comes into me.'

Love is thus the key to the mystery of <u>karma</u>; and it is our central assertion that the doctrine of Reincarnation is inadequate when confronted with the mystery of love.

The Doctrine of the Counterpartal Soul

At the heart of the doctrine of the Life-ray is the concept that the ego is bi-polar in structure. This may be called an archetypal fact of life.

Since the principle of positive and negative, male and female, active and passive, Yang and Yin runs through the whole universe, we must conceive of the Creator as 'Father-Mother', and not simply as 'Father'. And the self, as an expression of this transcendental life, must then also be dual in character. This is clearly stated in the Zohar, the basic text of Jewish mysticism.

'The world rests upon the union of the male with the female principle. That form in which we do not find the male and the female principle is neither a complete nor a superior form. The Holy One does not establish His residence in any place where such union does not exist. The name, Adam, was given to a man and a woman united as one sole being.'

If the basis of all creation be union between elements of an opposite polarity, then a person has spiritual as well as physical parents. These two lines of descent are in some way closely associated; a certain type of body, for instance, may be necessary to provide for certain spiritual experiences. But it is evidently possible for two individuals to have a similar biological origin and yet widely different spiritual affiliations, thus producing the startling contrasts between members of the same human family which are regarded by the reincarnationists as evidence of rebirth. The biologists have explored the way in which we inherit tendencies from our physical forebears. Now we may add the doctrine that our higher attainments are inherited from our spiritual forebears. These lofty beings are naturally impelled to watch over their spiritual children with a profound love, of which the love of earthly parents is but a pale reflection. And their deeds are reflected in the <u>karma</u> which the child bears in its earthly life.

The soul which has been brought into existence through the arcane spiritual union of the angelic parents is itself only one half of a complete being. For each of us there is a counterpartal ego of the opposite polarity. And our pilgrimage towards emancipation consists in drawing ever nearer to this balancing factor in our personality, so that in the end we become a male-female being in whom the positive and negative forces are in perfect equilibrium, reflecting the nature of the Male-Female Creator. Only through the perfect union of two souls of the opposite sex can that blending of forces be achieved which brings freedom from illusion and the full experience of Reality.

Repentance and Rectification

The reincarnationist may well confront the upholders of the doctrine of the Life Ray with a powerful argument; that what was set in motion on earth can only be rectified on earth. Sins committed when inhabiting a body must be expiated in a body; good deeds on earth produce good <u>karma</u> on earth. This implies that before we can gain release from the obligation to be reborn we must become absolute masters of the realm of earthly existence. The law of cause and effect is inescapable. If a vortex of life has been created by the human mind it will, through the activity of the <u>skandhas</u>, draw to itself again and again the appropriate spiritual atoms, repeatedly reproducing the original situation until negatived by a corresponding force. Nevertheless, it is also arguable that the complex of embodied forces created by an individual in a past epoch will not have to be dealt with exclusively by <u>that</u> <u>same</u> individual when it manifests again. The task of straightening out the original discords and perversions could fall to his successors on the Life Ray.

We do not learn only by the crude process of having birds 'come home to roost', or by realising that a certain type of conduct 'does not pay'. There is also the factor of illumination; when we enter the deeper spiritual states we perceive that a certain type of behaviour is wrong, and so identify ourselves with its opposite, and this can occur <u>before</u> the consequences of our wrong-doing are apparent to us. Spiritual discipline thus enables us to anticipate the painful realisations which would other-wise be brought home through the 'hard knocks' of fate. At present only a small minority of people are capable of dealing with their experiences on this level. The reincarnationists therefore understandably assert that rebirth is essential for our human education, since it is only by experiencing the physical effects of our actions that we can perceive where we have gone wrong. Having stolen, you will be at the mercy of thieves; having murdered, you will be murdered; having abused authority, you will yourself suffer the abuse of authority; and so on. The philosophical spiritualist, however, takes a different view. He believes that conditions in the 'next world' are more propitious for spiritual realisation than existence in a physical body. Moreover, since reincarnation is not involved, long periods of time – or what corresponds to time down here – are available for the soul's unfoldment. The combination of these two factors means that the individual may have come to understand and repent the actions of his early life long before the time has come for their renewed expression on earth. He has passed through the state known to Christians as Purgatory.

The spiritualist teaches that a clear distinction must be drawn between the <u>realisation</u> and the consequences of evil. After death the soul goes through a process of <u>judgement</u> as the automatic outworking of its past deeds – the concept of a stern Deity presiding over a Celestial Tribunal is, of course, a crude distortion of this interior spiritual process. Deep within, the soul knows that the indictment is unanswerable. And if the picture is grim, the sight of it fills him with <u>overwhelming remorse</u>. He understands now how he went wrong, and has an anguished longing to put things right. And equally he sees the fruit which his good deeds will bear in the future.

This vital principle means that instead of having the lessons of conscience brought home by the laborious process of renewed incarnation in a physical body, a person can realise the significance of his past deeds through direct spiritual contemplation. The confusion comes from fusing two distinct ideas; that we gain experience through our deeds; and that we must reap their consequences on the physical plane, that <u>after</u> he has perceived his mistakes, a person must again be blinded by the senses in order to suffer the consequences of what he has done, and so learn his lessons twice over.The problem disappears if we adopt the view that a person redeems his past by 'overshadowing' those called upon by Destiny to bear the reflex of his earthly acts.

The doctrine of the Life Ray is in accord with the doctrine of Reincarnation in assuming that the next act in the drama cannot be played until the exact combination of forces which inspired the previous act on the earth plane manifests again. But it then affirms that the burden is taken up on earth by another soul. Here we are brought face to face with the basic problem of 'justice'.

The Key to Unfoldment

As we have suggested earlier, the doctrine of Reincarnation cuts us off fatally from objective association with those in the inner spheres of being. The reincarnationists rightly perceive that there is no profit in intercourse with earth-bound spirits who are as ignorant and unenlightened as they were before death; the main significance of making contact with such beings is simply to establish the fact of Survival. Reincarnationists and Spiritualists both teach that the capacity of spirits who are withdrawing from the earth plane to communicate with humans diminishes as their minds turn to loftier states. The apparent degeneration of their powers is due to the fact that they are moving <u>away</u> from the conditions in which they were formerly active. According to the Theosophists, however, the movement of the soul after death is towards a state of subjectivity; it is preparing to enter the dream paradise of <u>Devachan</u>. According to the Spiritualists, its progress is towards a new mode of <u>objectivity</u> on a higher plane; the soul's evolution is accomplished by a series of embodiments in successively loftier modes of being. At some stage in the upward path the soul may well retire for a season into a subjective state. But the Spiritualists assert that if this occurs at all it is at a far higher stage in the long ascent than the Theosophists envisage, and that <u>in no case is withdrawal from the earth planes a prelude to re-embodiment</u>. According to many spirit communicators, when the process of dissociation from earth has been completed, 'the life power is exerted in the development and building up of the new succeeding form', a vehicle adapted to life in objective and vital terms on a new level of consciousness. This is of crucial importance, because the descent of life-power to man conforms to a hierarchical principle; it moves outwards from the innermost, through plane after plane of being, mediated by angelic personalities who were once mortals. And the most intimate and creative channels through which this life passes are those of a holy process of spiritual generation. We are brought back to the principle that power comes through love.

According to mystical philosophy, the association between spirits and mortals penetrates and transforms every aspect of man's life on earth. The experience of being subjectively attuned to forces operating upon the soul from the great Unseen cannot be fully explained by theories about the 'Unconscious'. What we think of as a psychological 'crisis' may in fact be a situation in which the discarnate and the incarnate are confronted with a problem which is of life-and-death importance to both, because the latter is carrying on a process initiated by the former.

We have already noted that when minds are in rapport or resonance with each other, the different locations of their 'bodies' or vehicles is irrelevant. The individuals concerned may be living thousands of miles apart on the earth plane, or some may be in physical form and others dwellers in some 'far off heaven'; yet because of their spiritual consubstantiality telepathic communication is easy. The human person may not register <u>consciously</u> the impulses reaching his mind from other planes, but they will penetrate his 'subconscious', and bear appropriate fruit. But it normally takes serious spiritual training to become capable of tuning in consciously to the inspiration of high-raised beings.

There is obviously a profound difference between the kind of telepathy practised by psychical investigators between humans, and the reception of impulses by humans from celestial beings. The thoughts projected by these beings to their kinsmen on earth are true 'inspiration'; they provide illumination, purification and guidance; the human receives a wonderful life-energy into his soul. And this communion occurs because both minds are attuned with a precision which is possibly only among members of the same spiritual family. The deepest link of all is that between the human and his or her angelic 'counterpart' or twin soul embodying the most fundamental form of love.

Conclusion: The Word and the Flesh

The doctrine of Reincarnation has disastrously <u>materialised</u> the doctrine of <u>karma</u>. It asserts that spirits can only 'return' by re-entering a series of wombs, and experiencing again and again an extreme form of limitation.

Of course the great ones of the past have come back to deal with the consequences of the deeds they did on earth. But they do so, not by reversing the spiritual current which is steadily carrying them into the realms of emancipation, but by inspiring their spiritual descendants from the high planes which they have now reached. They guide, enlighten, sustain and energise from afar – and yet in terms of profound intimacy and <u>rapport</u>. The conscious or unconscious identification between minds can be so complete that one can reproduce the thoughts and impulses of another. By this means art forms, philosophical doctrines, psychological attitudes and religious intuitions can be repeatedly manifested in the history of the world, appropriately clothed in the style of the period. This applies to both good and evil tendencies. The tremendous fact is that people can learn, through appropriate spiritual disciplines, to receive inspirationally the wisdom of those in the Unseen who have passed beyond the conceptions which they formulated on earth, and which are still conditioning the minds and deeds of their followers. Thus ancient errors are no longer repeated, and a new and higher light is given to the world. There is little spiritual profit in looking <u>backwards</u> to historical and traditional teachings. The creative thing is to look <u>upwards</u> and to attune oneself to the celestial spheres in which the ancient teachers now dwell.

There are important reasons why the channels of communication with the higher spiritual planes have hitherto been closed. First, for centuries the great traditional religions of the West, Christianity, Judaism and Islam, have taught little or nothing about the great world of the Unseen. The Hindus, the Buddhists and the Western esotericists, on the other hand, have almost all been uncritically attached to the theory of Reincarnation, which automatically cuts them off from objective association with celestial beings. Finally, the spiritualists, who have done a wonderful work in opening up contacts with the 'next world', have so far tended to tune in to regions close to the earth.

Nevertheless, the spiritualists are becoming increasingly aware that after death humans begin a long journey through a series of ever higher spiritual states, and that their guides and ministrants are themselves the instruments of higher beings. The door is thus opening to an advanced type of spiritualism, involving communion with celestial souls who have attained true angelhood.

CHAPTER 14

A Meeting With
Colin Fry

A meeting took place at the home of Chris and Hazel Hunt in East Sussex on 14th May 1995 with a gathering of people to listen to the mentor, known as 'Magnus', communicating from spirit through the well known and popular TV famed medium Colin Fry.

Myself (James Webster) and my wife Shirley were amongst the invited guests and a tape recording was taken of the proceedings.

The following is a transcript of exactly what Magnus had to say in answering a question on reincarnation:

Question from a gentleman: Good evening Magnus. We haven't met before. I have only been experiencing this kind of communication for less than a year, and before I became interested in it I had, all my adult life had a belief in reincarnation. It seemed a very natural and logical thing to be. I am now finding that spirit guides leave me to believe this is not the case and that I have been mistaken in this?

Magnus: You can only assess things from the amount of information that is provided to you, so I shouldn't castigate yourself with this. Reincarnation .... that abominable subject again! .... I shall probably say to you things you have not heard of, my friend. The spirit, the human spirit was, is and has forever been, designed for progression to experience the state of existence and with the understanding, move into a new state of existence and continually progress onwards. I have, with *The Diamond*, said before and I shall say again, the concept of reincarnation is not progression, it is regression. One cannot journey forward by continually going around and around in circles. Yes, you shall have knowledge of the earthplane beyond your morphic existence but it shall be as attachment. You, your spirit, your soul, your life-force will not occupy the earthplane again in morphic form. I recently heard an American lady speaking, and I rather liked her words – do you think it would be permissible to use them? (*response of 'yes'*)....... I heard an American lady speaking recently who said 'you only get one bite of the cookie' which I did not understand and had to ask for it to be explained to me. Once it had been explained I found it most amusing.

You shall have but one physical existence my friend. You will have morphic form but once.

Questioner: I understand. Could you say something about the term you used 'attachment' because I didn't quite understand that.

Magnus: You may of heard me speak earlier of the spirit being divisible. Once you have vacated morphic form you enter into a state of being where you are capable of being divisible, my friend. Spirit has sense of self that can be occupied in many things. I did at one time used to say 'at the same time'. The concept of time only applies upon the earthplane my friend, therefore I have stopped saying this. You can be occupied in many things at the single point – I think that's better. Part of this divisibility, my friend, remembering that there is no concept of time, is that part of your divided self, your divisibility, can form into attachment, can attach itself to the morphic existence of one that is travelling through the earthplane. Therefore you can observe their morphic life through their experiences. Some attachments have sufficient energies to be able to council to those they are attached, to subject their spirit to advice. So there will be situations in your existence where you will know how to deal with certain situations even though you have never encounted them and you may ask yourself; 'how did I know how to deal with that?' That is possibly the influence of the attachment. By the same token there are times when the attachment will flood the mind with knowledge of its own earthly experience and you will have memory of times gone by. This is why people believe that they remember former life. But be advised my friend, not all attachment is positive. There can be those that have attachment of negative aspects of the human spirit, of the human life force. Do you understand what I mean by this my friend?

Questioner: Yes I do Magnus.

Magnus: It is important to understand that the occupying spirit, <u>your</u> spirit, is the stronger. All other influences are but aspects – attachments – they do not have the full strength of an oversoul. Therefore if the occupying spirit is overpowered, it is because it does not understand or realise the potential of its own strength and that although attachments cannot be repelled, they can be subdued and silenced. But you must understand that most attachments are merely observers and many on occasions be able to influence and advise the spirit and at times influence the mind so that knowledge of their own earthly morphic existence may be known. Do you understand what I have said my friend?

Questioner: Yes you have made it very clear Magnus. Thank you.

Magnus: And you would still have those that say to you my friend, even from our side of existence, you must have many earthly lives before you can progress. I have not been in the state of spirit for so many years as some that communicate, but I am an aspect, I am a member of *The Diamond* and therefore my knowledge extends through their grace many many thousands of your earthly years. I know of no aspect or member of *The Diamond* that has had more than one morphic existence. I have not encountered any being in the state of spirit that has reincarnated, but I have encountered many who are awaiting reincarnation. I do hope this helps you with your enquiry my friend.

Questioner: Yes it does. It's quite a big jump. A mental jump to me.

Magnus: You must understand that the concept of reincarnation, just as when I spoke to this young man, our young friend, about energies of ancient times, the concept of reincarnation was for a time that has gone by.

It enabled human spirit, morphic beings of that time, to make sense of their existence and their place in the Universe. It helped them to develop a discipline and a code of practice to govern their morphic existence and does not, as many things of ancient times that have been put aside mean that they were right. In times gone by there were those that would rip from the morphic body of their fellows the heart and offer it to the sun. In your modern times would you wish this practice to take place? There are things of history, of the past, that reach a point of understanding when they must be put aside. The concept of reincarnation is for a time that has been and gone and the human spirit in morphic form has developed onwards since this point – not in all aspects I would say. But this concept should now be put to rest and a new and advanced and developed understanding of your spirit must now occupy your minds.

With your permission my friend I shall move on .... let us move on.

CHAPTER 15

Cartoons

When presenting my various talks and lectures, I often include some cartoons to lighten the proceedings. These are projected onto a screen before the audience.

My brother Tony is a very talented artist and between us we have produced a fine selection of original cartoons. I present the ideas and captions and Tony does the artwork in his unique style. The cartoons I have included in this book will, I hope, illustrate how a picture can speak more than a thousand words! I hope the reader will be amused and at the same time accept the importance of the intended message.

<u>Mabel:</u> No ... Fred's not going to a fancy dress party. He's off to work as usual. Problem is, he's now convinced he was a famous warrior in a past life!

"You and your beloved husband will meet again on the same path after your next three reincarnations ...... but as brother and sister and as opposite gender"

<u>CLERK</u>: We are completely over-booked on Napoleon, Anne of Cleaves and Joan of Arc .... How does Atilla the Hun grab you?

THIEF: Don't you arrest me! These belonged to me in my last incarnation.

<u>Reincarnationist Medium</u>: I have good news and bad news for you. The good news is that you will soon pass into a much better world free of all pain and suffering .... The bad news is that you will reincarnate to pay off some more karmic debts.

<u>New Arrival:</u> Please take me to meet my dear wife at last.
<u>St. Peter:</u> Sorry you are just too late. She has reincarnated as your grandson.

<u>Clerk</u>: You will be a Gigolo next time.
<u>Old Lady</u>: Oh, is that one of those foreigners, and is it being of service?

Client: I feel sure I was Florence Nightingale in a past life.
Medium: Oh, but Florence communicates regularly through our home circle.

Client: I am getting a burning feeling in my chest.
Medium: I sense that you were burnt at the stake as a witch in a past life.
Client: I think it could be the curry I had for lunch.

CHAPTER 16

In Conclusion

I trust the reader has stayed the course of this book and we can share a few final thoughts together.

Hopefully from reading and digesting the contents, all will have a clearer understanding, and emerge from the maze somewhat relieved, without the overhanging fears and uncertainties they might have been living with due to the complex problems associated with reincarnation belief. There will, of course, be those – and I mean particularly the 'hard-boiled reincarnationists' who hate any form of criticism of their belief – who will try their upmost to find a way out of their corner. I am sure that the intelligent thinking person will have no difficulty in deciding which side of the fence they find themselves comfortable with.

It has been made clear from the evidence shown in the chapters of this book that what has been, and is being accepted, as reincarnation and past-lives is unreliable and unscientific and breaks natural law.

When one considers that all alleged cases of past life recall could have any of the following explanations, it becomes quite impossible for any thinking person to accept the doctrine of reincarnation as being a fact or truth:

1. Cryptomnesia*
2. Confabulation**

3. Obsession or possession
4. Overshadowing
5. Hypnotic suggestibility
6. Auto-hypnosis
7. Astral projection
8. Out-of-body experience (OBE)
9. Mind before brain (déjà vu)
10. Genetic memory
11. Being psychic or mediumistic without realising it
12. Tapping into the collective unconscious sometimes referred to as the Akashic records
13. The use of drugs and other medicaments

Cryptomnesia ...... Photo reading into the subconscious e.g. glancing at a page in a book or just flicking through the pages, maybe many years ago, perhaps at a library. The subconscious stores the information which the conscious mind is unaware of until such time or moment that it registers for some reason.

A person may believe that they have been a famous historical character or that they were of a different race in another country in an alleged past life because of some attraction and interest in that person or period of history or part of the world, perhaps when they were a child at school. The imagination can create and store into the subconscious.

**Confabulation* ...... To replace FACT with FANTASY in memory.*

A word of warning when booking to have a sitting with a *medium* or *psychic*. Find out first, before parting with your money, if they accept reincarnation and past lives or are mixed up with other *new-age* money making rackets otherwise you are more likely get a whole load of unreliable information impossible to prove, simply to flatter the ego!

What others have quoted:

- *If reincarnation was factual it would be spiritual abortion and new souls would have little or no opportunity of crystallizing.*
- *It may be impossible to prove a negative but as there is no evidence to prove reincarnation that in itself provides the answer.*
- *Reincarnation has become the pornography of Spiritualism.*

American psychiatrist Prof. Ian Stevenson is often referred to by reincarnationists as an 'authority'. His name has cropped up in this book but there are plenty of references to his work available. Although many respect his research – including myself – perhaps it was a pity that he didn't follow closer to his mother's belief in spiritualism and become more familiar with the philosophy of spiritualism and survival rather than to persue – somewhat dogmatically in my opinion – reincarnation, using his intellectual and academic background to try and find some kind of scientific proof for the theory. He admitted that he had not found a 'watertight case' in spite of the many years and great efforts he put into his research.

I have to insist that the proof for survival and the continuation of life cannot be uncovered with reincarnation research, belief or following. It is an erroneous route to take – a distraction leading into 'cul-de-sacs'.

Another useful reference book worth a mention which covers many popular cases often cited by reincarnationists is: *MIND OUT OF TIME? Reincarnation Claims Investigated* by Ian Wilson (Published 1981 Victor Gallancz Ltd). The reader will find much information on for example: The Briday Murphy Case, Arnall Bloxham, Joe Keeton, Prof. Ian Stevenson. Hypnotic Regression. Multiple Personality.

For those of my readers who own or have access to a computer I would recommend they put into their search engine *Shopping For Spirit – The Search For Truth* by Steve Gamble. This is a masterpiece requiring much to read and comprehend. Each chapter is almost a book in itself. Steve makes clear with his historical references together with his own meditations and deep research how misconceptions are deceiving the world. Like the stage magician leading the audience along with clever deception and illusion. Many will be shocked, angered or disturbed by it, but the warning is clear that reincarnation belief is bound up with those who are intent, by whatever means, to keep us earthbound, in ignorance, and in their total control by attempting and confusing, to prevent us from natural spiritual progression through the Light. I have enjoyed a number of long telephone conversations with Steve and keep in touch with him over such controversial issues.

For obvious reasons it would be a far safer and wiser choice to leave this world holding a non-belief in reincarnation, or at least an open minded attitude, rather than the dogmatic one of <u>attachment</u> to the theory or doctrine. We take all our beliefs and ideas with us.

'As a man thinketh, so is he'.

Bibliography & References

Bahá'í Faith, *Some Answered Questions (U.S. Bahá'í Publishing Trust 1990)*

Beetham, Ken, *Just Thoughts (Kaymar Press)*

Boddington, Harry, *The University of Spiritualism (First impression 1947 – Latest impression 2002 Psychic Press (1995) Ltd)*

Buddington, Thomas Cushman, *Illuminated Brahmanism (Spiritual Scientific Publication Co. 1889)*

Campbell Praed, Mrs., *Soul of Nyria* – The memory of a past life in ancient Rome (Rider, London 1931)

Cerminara, Dr. D.R. Gina, *Many Mansions – The Edgar Cayce Story on Reincarnation (Penguin Books Australia Ltd. 1990)*

Cockell, Jenny, *Yesterday's Children (Piatkus Publishers Ltd. 1993)*

Conan Doyle, Sir Arthur, *The History of Spiritualism Volume Two (First impression 1926 – later impression 1989 Psychic Press Ltd)*

Ellison, Prof. Arthur J., *Science and the Paranormal (Floris Books 2003)*

Gamble, Steve, *Shopping For Spirit – The Search for Truth (Ref: Equilibra website on the internet)*

Greater World Christian Spiritualist Association, The, *The Zodiac Messages – Reference Edition (The Greater World Association first published 1965, reprinted 1978, 1988, 1991)*

Hinnells, John R., *A Handbook of Living Religions (Penguin Books Ltd. 1991)*

Huxley, Aldous, *Perennial Philosophy (Chatto & Windus 1946 UK 1st Edition – Later Edition Perennial 1990)*

Hyde, Lawrence, *The Learned Knife (G. Howe Ltd. London 1928); The Prospects of Humanism (G. Howe Ltd. London 1931); Isis and Osiris (Kessinger Publishing 1948); The Nameless Faith (Rider & Co. London 1949); Spirit and Society (The Omega Press, Reigate, Surrey 1953); I Who Am (The Omega Press,Reigate, Surrey 1954); An Introduction to OrganicPhilosophy: An essay on the reconciliation of the masculine and feminine principles (The Omega Press, Reigate, Surrey 1955)*

Kardec, Allan, *The Spirits' Book (First published 1857 by Allan Kardec. Reprinted in 2006 by Cosimo Inc.); The Medium's Book (First published 1861 by Allan Kardec. Softback editions reprinted 1987, 1998)*

Krishnamurti, Jiddu, *Questions and Answers (Jan. 1982 The Krishnamurti Foundation Trust Ltd.)*

Morse, Dr. Melvin, *Where God Lives (Morse, 2000)*

Merrill, Rev. Joseph H. *Do I Have To Return? (Ref: Lily Dale Assembly, USA)*

Olcott, Colonel, *Old Diary Leaves (Refs: Theosophical Publishing Society/House 1895-1935)*

Oram, Arthur, *The System In Which We Live (Talbot Books 1998)*

Ross, Alan, *Spiritualism And Beyond (Ross Publications 2004)*

Sagan, Prof. Carl, *The Demon-Haunted World (Ballantine Books 1997)*

Shakespeare, William, *The Phoenix and the Turtle (poem)*

Spence, Lewis, *Encyclopaedia of Occultism (Citadel 1984)*

Tweedale, Rev. Charles L., *Man's Survival After Death (Grant Richards Ltd. First Edition 1909 Second Edition 1920); News From The Next World (T. Werner Laurie Ltd. Second Edition 1940)*

Waterlow, Charlotte, *The Mystery of Karma – Reincarnation or Ray-Incarnation? (abridged and edited version); The Hinge of History (The One World Trust 1995)*

Wickland, Dr. Carl A., *Thirty Years Among The Dead (First published 1924. Further edition by Spiritualist Press 1971); The Gateway Of Understanding (National Psychological Institute Inc. 1934)*

Wilson, Ian, *Mind Out Of Time (Victor Gollancz Ltd. 1981)*

Index